# POETRY HACKS

The ultimate student guide to poetic features
and how to write about them

J. E. CLAPHAM

# Contents

# Introduction

If you're about to write an essay on a poem – a commentary, an appreciation, an unseen poetry analysis – then you must begin by **reading** and **re-reading** the text, annotating the text with features, with your thoughts, and picking out phrases that catch your eye. Make sure, before going any further, that you give some thought to what the poem is about, i.e. what the poem is exploring or communicating (ideas, feelings).

**Poetry Hacks** is to help you with *the next stage*.

Now that you have noticed some features (poetic techniques, devices, tropes) what can you say about them? There are lots of glossaries of literary terms available, but often it's more helpful to read about the **effects** produced by these features.

This book can teach you about nearly a hundred poetic features, with definitions and discussion of the effects they produce, both in general terms and in relation to specific **examples**. Don't worry about the more obscure terms on the list: the golden rule is that you should use the terms that are *useful* for the text in hand.

After the alphabetical list of features, there are some **longer explanations**, giving help with the complicated terminology surrounding versification, describing the sounds of words, and with writing skills that my students have often found useful in the past.

# Accumulatio

**What is it?**
Piling up accusation or praise towards the end of a text, to summarise points made earlier.

**What effect does it usually have?**
Like other listing devices, accumulatio usually has the effect of quickening the pace.

**What else should I look out for?**
Usually accumulatio creates a sense of building intensity.

**An example of how it works …**
'To S. and C.' by P. B. Shelley:

> .. *two vultures sick for battle, / Two scorpions under one wet stone, / Two bloodless wolves whose dry throats rattle, / Two crows perched on the murrained cattle, / Two vipers tangled into one.*

Shelley expresses his contempt for the Tory politicians addressed in the poem using a rapid sequence of animal metaphors, closing the poem with the most graphic and disturbing.

# Alexandrine

See: Long Line

# Allegory

See: Personification

# Alliteration

**What is it?**
Where two or more nearby words begin with the same consonant sound.

**What effect does it usually have?**
Words are given greater emphasis by being **alliterated**, and connected to one another, creating a strong sense of cohesion or harmony; certain sounds, which might have an onomatopoeic or other effect, are also made more noticeable.

**What else should I look out for?**
Since alliteration was used instead of rhyme in Old English poetry (e.g. in *Beowulf*), where two or three words are alliterated every line, poets sometimes use it to evoke the Dark Ages.

**An example of how it works …**
'Sonnet 127' by William Shakespeare:

*Fairing the foul with Art's false borrowed face*

In this line, the poet expresses his contempt for the use of heavy make-up: those who are naturally ugly ('foul') can paint themselves a more attractive ('fair') face. The alliteration binds the operative words of the line together, giving special emphasis to the fourth alliterated word, 'false'; this is especially important, since a key idea of the poem is the contrast between the beloved's true beauty and the artificial – and temporary ('borrowed') – beauty of other women.

**Another example …**
'The Shadow on the Stone' by Thomas Hardy:

*I thought her behind my back,*
*Yea, her I long had learned to lack*

Here the poet remembers his wife Emma while visiting the Druid Stone; he feels sure her ghost is standing behind him. The pronounced alliteration in these (and many other) lines helps him conjure up a mysterious setting, suiting both the eerie feeling he describes as well as the idea that the past is always with us.

# Allusion

**What is it?**
A reference, usually to a literary, mythological or religious text.

**What effect does it usually have?**
Allusions carry a range of associations that enrich what is being described with additional ideas or feelings; depending on the text **alluded** to, they can also lend the poem a sense of dignity, weight, seriousness, importance, etc.

**What else should I look out for?**
Very **allusive** texts tend to build a relationship between the poet and the reader, since they assume a shared culture or style of education; conversely, they often also make poems richer and more ambiguous, especially when allusions are left unexplained (e.g. in *The Cantos* by Ezra Pound).

**An example of how it works …**
'Ode to a Nightingale' by John Keats:

> *Perhaps [this is] the self-same song that found a path*
> *Through the sad heart of Ruth, when, sick for home,*
> *She stood in tears amid the alien corn*

Here Keats refers to Ruth from the Old Testament, whom he imagines to be comforted by the same birdsong as she longs for distant places with an aching heart. The allusion supports the key idea from the first line of the stanza: the nightingale is 'immortal', above the pain of human life.

# Anaphora

**What is it?**
Where a word or short phrase is repeated at the start of consecutive lines, sentences, or clauses.

**What effect does it usually have?**
Anaphora is a simple structuring device, like listing; it may create a sense of urgency and an assertive or insistent tone.

**What else should I look out for?**
Very often anaphora builds tension and may be used to create an emotional climax.

**An example of how it works …**
'London' by William Blake:

> *Marks of weakness, marks of woe*

Here anaphora is used within a single line, implying that all the poet 'marks' (sees) in the streets of London are weakness and 'woe' (suffering) – nothing else – an effect heightened by the use of alliteration on 'w'.

**Another example …**
'London' by William Blake:

> *In every cry of every Man,*
> *In every Infants cry of fear,*
> *In every voice: in every ban,*
> *The mind-forged manacles I hear*

In this stanza, which follows straight after the example above, the poet gives examples of the 'weakness' and 'woe' he sees (a 'ban' is a curse). The word 'every' is repeated **anaphorically** to make the conclusion in the fourth line even more forceful: all of the suffering is caused by the people of London being mentally chained up ('manacled') – one of the key ideas of the poem.

# Anthimeria

**What is it?**
Where a word that is usually a noun is used as a verb; where one part of speech is substituted for another (more accurately).

**What effect does it usually have?**
Anthimeria creates a sense of surprise, creativity, or originality.

**What else should I look out for?**
The use of anthimeria implies that the usual words would fail to do justice to what is being described by the writer, such is its beauty, intensity, or uniqueness.

**An example of how it works …**
'To a Sky-Lark' by P. B. Shelley:

> *The blue deep thou wingest,*
> *And singing still dost soar*

In the poet's vision, the bird flies ('wings') in the 'blue deep' of the sky, near to heaven; the use of anthimeria makes it seem less like a common bird, and more like a joyous 'spirit' or angel.

**Another example …**
'Spring Offensive' by Wilfred Owen:

> *.. the green slope*
> *Chasmed and deepened sheer to infinite space*

These remarkable lines describe the ground literally turning to air beneath feet of the charging soldiers as the 'hot blast' of explosions carry them into the air. The use of anthimeria creates a sense of normality being replaced by a strange and hellish nightmare.

# Anthropomorphism

**What is it?**
Giving animals or other non-human things human characteristics.

**What effect does it usually have?**
Anthropomorphism is a way both of visualising and making ideas more accessible to readers.

**What else should I look out for?**
Some uses of anthropomorphism contribute to presenting the speaker as naïve or child-like; others come across as sentimental, especially where furry animals are involved, resulting in a comic effect.

**An example of how it works ...**
'Time and Eternity, V' by Emily Dickinson:

> *The birds rose smiling in their nests*
> *The gales indeed were done*

The poet anthropomorphises the birds' faces to forge a connection between the animal world and the human world, implying that all living things feel relief at the passing of the storm.

**Another example ...**
'Sonnet 97' by William Shakespeare:

> *Leaves look pale dreading winter's near*

The idea of leaves becoming pale with the dread of winter (after hearing the cheerless singing of the birds, no less) seems on first sight to be an example of anthropomorphism taken to ridiculous extremes. However, the principal theme of this poem is the psychological impact of separation; as Helen Vendler puts it, the poem as a whole 'wilfully confuses' imagined appearance and 'evidential reality'; this final line acts as further evidence that the speaker's 'wintry' emotional state has affected his perception of everything in the world around him.

# Antithesis

**What is it?**
The use of opposites to structure a phrase or line; a thematic contrast.

**What effect does it usually have?**
Antithesis emphasises ideas; it often creates a balanced, elegant phrase.

**What else should I look out for?**
Since it often involves contrasting imagery, antithesis tends to make poems more vivid. Whole poems can sometimes be based around an antithesis.

**An example of how it works …**
'After a Journey' by Thomas Hardy:

> *Summer gave us sweets, but autumn wrought division*

Here the poet sets up an antithesis between the happy youth of his marriage (summer) on the one hand, and the unhappy later years (autumn); the comma neatly 'divides' this phrase in two halves, rather like the marriage itself.

**Another example …**
'Sonnet 50' by William Shakespeare:

> *My grief lies onward, and my joy behind*

This elegantly balanced phrase is built around a binary opposition: ahead is unhappiness (grief); behind is happiness (joy). It seems the perfect last line for a poem all about the misery of having to take a journey away from the beloved.

# Apostrophe

**What is it?**
Where the speaker addresses an absent person, an idea or an object (e.g. Juliet's last three lines are an apostrophe addressed to her dagger).

**What effect does it usually have?**
Apostrophes can lend high emotion to the climax of a narrative; because they are an important convention of classical rhetoric, they tend to make poems in English sound elevated, formal, grand and 'classical'. Apostrophes are often also used to give lyrical poems an arresting opening.

**What else should I look out for?**
The self-consciously poetic and artificial nature of apostrophe—after all, no one sane **apostrophizes** in real life—means that many poets include apostrophe for comic effect or in a playful or mocking way.

**An example of how it works ...**
*The Prelude* by William Wordsworth:

> *O, ye rocks and streams,*
> *and that still spirit of the evening air,*
> *Even in this time I felt your presence*

Here the poet addresses the environment of his childhood to convey his intimate relationship with the natural world.

**Another example ...**
*Don Juan*, Canto II by Lord Byron:

> *Oh, Love! Of whom great Caesar was the suitor,*
> *Titus the master, Anthony the slave,*
> *...Oh, Love! Thou art the very god of evil*

*For, after all, we cannot call thee devil.*

These lines introduce a long and witty digression on deception in love that forms part of the climax of Canto II; the histrionic, excessive style of the passage suggests that Byron does not want us to take him entirely seriously.

# Archaism

**What is it?**
The use of words in a form of English no longer spoken in everyday life.

**What effect does it usually have?**
Archaisms helps to enhance the setting when poems are set in the distant past; poets sometimes use archaism to bring their style closer to that of great poets that they admire.

**What else should I look out for?**
Most contemporary poets keep their language close to contemporary, spoken English; archaism tends to be used playfully, for humorous effect, or in very specific situations.

**An example of how it works …**
'The Eve of St Agnes' by John Keats:

> *I've mickle time to grieve*

Here an old man says that he has 'mickle' (i.e. plenty of) time for grieving. In 1819, when this line was written, the word 'mickle' had been out of general use for over two hundred years. Keats uses it, along with other archaisms, to enhance the medieval setting of the poem.

**Another example …**
'Parable of the Old Man and the Young' by Wilfred Owen:

> *Isaac the first-born spake and said, My Father*

Here the poet uses an archaic past tense form of 'speak' because he is imitating the style of the King James translation of the Bible, which was written three hundred years before the poem.

# Aspirants

**What is it?**
Using a number of words close together containing an aspirant (spelt h in Standard English). See Describing Sound in Poetry.

**What effect does it usually have?**
Like fricatives, aspirants have a soft sound that is useful for poets seeking to evoke pleasant settings, or to give the music of their writing a warm, pretty quality.

**What else should I look out for?**
Aspirants are often used onomatopoeically to represent breathing or a gentle breeze.

**An example of how it works …**
*The Prelude* by William Wordsworth:

> *Still hurrying hurrying onward, how my heart*
> *Panted*

Here aspirant alliteration is used to mimic the breathless panting of the child-poet as he ran on the hillsides catching birds.

**Another example …**
'Sonnet 22' by William Shakespeare:

> *when her mournful hymns did hush the night*

In this fittingly musical line, the poet recalls the song of the nightingale during summer nights. The three aspirants work in harmony with nasal consonance and soft fricatives to create a wistful beauty.

# Assonance

### What is it?
Where vowel sounds are repeated in words that are near to one another in a poem.

### What effect does it usually have?
Assonance creates a sense of harmony, cohesion, and of words belonging together; it also emphasises important words.

### What else should I look out for?
Like rhyme and consonance, assonance is often used to bind lines together, or to connect related words to create a resonant, memorable phrase. The repetition of longer vowels usually slows the pace of a poem (see Describing Sound in Poetry).

### An example of how it works …
'Sonnet 12' by William Shakespeare:

> *When lofty trees I see barren of leaves*
> *Which erst from heat did canopy the herd*

In these perfectly musical lines, 'trees', 'see', 'leaves' and 'heat' all **assonate** on their long vowel, helping to create a sense of longing for the bright summer of youth. The beauty of the lines is rounded off by the assonance of 'herd' both with 'erst' (meaning 'in the past') and its alliteration with 'heat'.

### Another example …
'After a Journey' by Thomas Hardy:

> *autumn wrought division*

Here the poet reflects on how his relationship with Emma deteriorated in the later years of his life (the 'autumn' years). The assonance on 'autumn' and 'wrought' emphasises this key phrase, at the same time implying that it was their age, rather than his or her behaviour, that was responsible for what he - rather euphemistically - calls their 'division'.

# Asyndetic List

**What is it?**
A list without 'and' (or any other conjunction).

**What effect does it usually have?**
The absence of words connecting the items in a list tends to quicken the pace, enhancing the text's dramatic impact.

**What else should I look out for?**
In some cases, e.g. where a poet lists a series of significant objects, adjectives, or adverbs, there is a greater separation between the listed items, and each takes on greater significance.

**An example of how it works …**
*Don Juan*, Canto II by Lord Byron:

> *Strange sounds of wailing, blasphemy, devotion*
> *Clamoured in chorus to the roaring ocean*

The frantic behaviour of passengers aboard a sinking ship is described with greater intensity by listing the sounds that could be heard **asyndetically**.

**Another example …**
'The Convergence of the Twain' by Thomas Hardy:

> *Over the mirrors …*
> *The sea-worm crawls—grotesque, slimed, dumb, indifferent*

Imagining the lavish interiors of the Titanic now at the bottom of the Atlantic, Hardy uses an asyndetic list for a shocking portrayal of its new inhabitants.

# Asyndeton

**What is it?**
Where a series of phrases or lines are written without the usual conjunctions between them (and, but, or, nor, yet, so, etc.).

**What effect does it usually have?**
Asyndeton tends to create a more dense, concentrated style; it is a form of ellipsis. It can make a poem feel tougher or colder in tone.

**What else should I look out for?**
Without conjunctions, the reader is often left to understand for themselves how phrases or lines are related to one another, or the connection between them.

**An example of how it works ...**
'Homecoming' by Langston Hughes:

> *I opened up my door.*
> *All her clothes was gone:*
> *She wasn't home no more.*
> *I pulled back the covers,*
> *I made down the bed.*
> *A whole lot of room.*
> *Was the only thing I had.*

Here the asyndeton, combined with the simple diction and lack of imagery, conveys the speaker's sense of emptiness as he confronts the stark reality of abandonment.

**Another example ...**
'The Auguries of Innocence' by William Blake:

> *The Strongest Poison ever known*

*Came from Caesar's Laurel Crown*
*Nought can Deform the Human Race*
*Like to the Armour's iron brace*
*When Gold & Gems adorn the Plow*
*To peaceful Arts shall Envy Bow*

These lines are taken from a poem made up of over a hundred lines of proverbs, one after the other, with very little conjunction and no punctuation. The first four lines refer to the moral corruption caused by greed for wealth and power, and the wars caused by that greed. One way to interpret the proverb of the fifth and sixth lines is that it offers an alternative to empire and military conquest, but the lack of conjunction makes it impossible to be sure. Blake's use of asyndeton heightens the ambiguity of the poem, making it more enigmatic, more fascinating.

# Blazon

**What is it?**
Where a woman's attractive physical features (hair, forehead, lips, teeth, neck, etc.) are described one after the other, normally using hyperbolic simile and metaphor with anaphora.

**What effect does it usually have?**
Reducing women to an 'inventory' of beautiful objects is generally repugnant to modern readers. In the past blazons were presumably intended to demonstrate the ingenuity of the poet; they give later poetry formal, artificial air, and evoke the distant world of the Elizabethan court.

**What else should I look out for?**
Even in Elizabethan times, blazons were thought clichéd and absurd – Shakespeare, Greene and Sidney mock them very amusingly; most post-Elizabethan examples are written in the spirit of fun and parody.

**An example of how it works …**
'Epithalamion' by Edmund Spenser:

> *Her goodly eyes like sapphires shining bright,*
> *Her forehead ivory white,*
> *Her cheeks like apples which the sun hath rudded,*
> *Her lips like cherries charming men to bite,*
> *Her breast like to a bowl of cream …*

These lines – from a blazon more than twice this length – present the body of the bride as a valuable commodity to be bought, admired for its outward charms, and then consumed.

**Another example …**
*Don Juan*, Canto II by Lord Byron:

> *Her glossy hair was cluster'd o'er a brow*
> *Bright with intelligence, and fair, and smooth;*
> *Her eyebrow's shape was like th' aerial bow,*
> *Her cheek all purple with the beam of youth …*

Here we first encounter Haidée; the use of blazon establishes her as an ideal 'damsel', a child of nature in contrast to women that have been corrupted by society. Although Byron avoids the excesses of hyperbole, the effect of the blazon still feels somewhat overdone, preparing us for Don Juan's admiration of her in the coming stanzas.

# Block Form

**What is it?**
Where a poem is written as a single block of text, rather than being divided into stanzas.

**What effect does it usually have?**
Poems in block form tend to feel heavier and more intense; block form also helps create a strong sense of cohesion.

**What else should I look out for?**
Since English sonnets tend to be written in block form, poems of a similar, but longer or shorter, length tend to resemble sonnets when laid out this way.

**An example of how it works …**
'The Young Bride' by Langston Hughes:

> *They say she died—I do not know,*
> *They say she died of grief*
> *And in the earth-dark arms of Death*
> *Sought calm relief,*
> *And rest from pain of love*
> *In loveless sleep*

In this one-sentence poem, Hughes uses block form to create a fitting weight and seriousness, in spite of its short lines and overall brevity.

# Bob Line

See: Short Line

# Caesura

## What is it?
A pause within a line of verse, rather than (or as well as) the pause expected at the end. Although some argue that nearly all lines of reasonable length contain one or more **caesuras**, it is usually best to use the term with more significant pauses.

Some critics find it useful to distinguish different types: a **masculine caesura** follows a stressed syllable; a **feminine caesura** follows an unstressed syllable; an **initial caesura** comes near the start of a line; a **medial caesura** comes around the middle (which is typical); and a **terminal caesura** comes near the end of a line.

## What effect does it usually have?
The regular placement of caesuras may be used to give further structure to lines of verse, as with Old English poetry (where medial caesuras are a formal requirement). Elsewhere, poets use caesuras in different positions to create a sense of variety, unpredictability or to make the verse seem less stiff and more speech-like—indeed, caesuras are often found alongside other irregular verse features, such as enjambment, creating a sense of disorder. See Understanding Versification and Rocking Lineation.

## What else should I look out for?
Since it 'cuts' across the line, an individual caesura will often emphasise an important word or image, or may be used mimetically to portray something faltering (as in Robert Frost's phrase 'little—less—nothing' to describe the stopping of a heart).

## An example of how it works …
'An Essay on Man' by Alexander Pope:

> *Man walked with beast, joint tenant of the shade;*
> *The same his table, and the same his bed;*
> *No murder clothed him, and no murder fed.*

Here the poet evokes a Golden Age in which man lived alongside animals without feeling the need to kill them for meat or fur. 'The state of Nature was the reign of God' he says, and the lines have a suitably balanced, calm, rational quality enhanced by each pentameter being neatly halved using a caesura.

### Another example …
'Sonnet 73' by William Shakespeare:

> *That time of year thou mayst in me behold*
> *When yellow leaves, or none, or few do hang*
> *Upon those boughs which shake against the cold*

In comparing his ageing self to a tree in winter, the speaker uses two caesuras in quick succession after an enjambed line containing none. This places emphasis on the shaking leaves and makes them seem sparse and somehow pitiful.

# Chiasmus

**What is it?**

Repeating words or phrases in reverse order, creating an ABBA pattern (e.g. 'I wasted time and now doth time waste me.') Stanzas and indeed whole texts can have a **chiastic structure**, where images and other elements are repeated to make the same pattern.

**What effect does it usually have?**

Chiasmus makes poems look carefully constructed, elegant and balanced.

**What else should I look out for?**

Since a good chiasmus is not easy to write, they can make a text seem witty, ingenious, even showy or contrived. The more compressed examples of chiasmus, where words are repeated very close together, sometimes create a feeling of crowding or entrapment.

**An example of how it works ...**

'The Eve of St Agnes' by John Keats:

> *They glide, like phantoms, into the wide hall;*
> *Like phantoms, to the iron porch they glide*

The use of chiasmus creates a sense of calm and serenity, helping to bring the poem to a peaceful resolution, as the lovers creep past the drunken guards and disappear into the night.

**Another example ...**

'Sonnet 28' by William Shakespeare:

> *When day's oppression is not eased by night,*
> *But day by night and night by day oppressed*

The chiastic repetition of the words 'day' and 'night' from the previous line present the speaker as unable to escape his obsession: the tormented lover never finds any relief, since Night and Day have joined forces to 'torture' him.

# Closed Couplet

### What is it?
Two consecutive lines that rhyme and together make up an entire sentence.

### What effect does it usually have?
Closed couplets are neat, concise, polished; they make the idea being expressed sound more convincing, as well as more memorable.

### What else should I look out for?
When closed couplets are used one after the other, they tend to become separate units, and take on individual importance.

### An example of how it works ...
'Auguries of Innocence' by William Blake:

> *A dog starved at his master's gate*
> *Predicts the ruin of the state*

In this neat and resonant closed couplet, the poet expresses the idea that cruelty to animals indicates a dangerous moral decline in society. The rhyme reinforces the poet's cause-effect logic: the cruelty in the first line seems to lead inevitably to the 'ruin' of the second.

# Coinage

**What is it?**
The use of a newly-invented word or phrase. Also called a
**neologism**.

**What effect does it usually have?**
The use of a coinage is striking or surprising; it implies that
what is being described is so exceptional that the existing
words of English are inadequate.

**What else should I look out for?**
Coinages are sometimes portmanteau words (i.e. created by
combining two existing words).

**An example of how it works …**
'On Seeing a Heavy Piece of Artillery Brought into Action'
by Wilfred Owen:

> *Be not withdrawn, dark arm, thy spoilure done,*
> *Safe to the bosom of our prosperity*

Here the poet **coins** the word 'spoilure' to refer to the
unprecedented destruction he expects the gun to wreak upon
the enemy, after which it must be destroyed. The coinage
appears to be a combination of 'spoil' and 'failure'.

# Comparative

### What is it?
Grammatical term for the type of adjective or adverb ending in '-er' (brighter, faster, better, etc.)

### What effect does it usually have?
Like superlatives, comparatives are often used to reinforce a sense of excellence; they are therefore frequently used when praising (or flattering) a loved one, or when invoking a divinity.

### What else should I look out for?
A string of comparatives may be used, or the same comparative anaphorically, to suggest that the poet is overcome with admiration.

### An example of how it works …
'Sonnet 91' by William Shakespeare:

> *Thy love is better than high birth to me,*
> *Richer than wealth, prouder than garments' cost,*
> *Of more delight than hawks and horses be*

Here the speaker assures the beloved that his love is superior to the pleasures enjoyed by princes using an elegant tricolon; the comparatives carry the additional implication that his love is ennobling.

### Another example …
'Ode to Psyche' by John Keats:

> *Fairer than Phoebe's sapphire-regioned star,*
> *Or Vesper, amorous glow-worm of the sky;*
> *Fairer than these, though temple thou hast none,*
> *Nor altar heaped with flowers*

The comparative 'fairer' is repeated anaphorically to stress the peerless beauty of Psyche, which exceeds both that of the moon (Phoebe's star) and of the Evening Star (Vesper) even though the ancients never built her a temple. These allusions connect Psyche both with chastity (via Phoebe and the moon, associated with Artemis) and with erotic love (via Venus, the other name for Vesper), whilst implying that she is brighter than both of them.

# Consonance

**What is it?**
Where consonant sounds are repeated mid-word or at the end of words that are near to one another in a poem.

**What effect does it usually have?**
Consonance creates a sense of harmony, cohesion, and of words belonging together; many contemporary poets use consonance on end-words, for a more subtle effect than full rhyme.

**What else should I look out for?**
Like rhyme and assonance, consonance is often used to bind lines together, or to connect related words to create a resonant, memorable phrase. The repetition of consonant sounds can produce various effects, depending on nature of the sounds being repeated (see Describing Sound in Poetry).

**An example of how it works …**
'The Fly' by William Blake:

> *For I dance*
> *And drink and sing,*
> *Till some blind hand*
> *Shall brush my wing*

Here the nasal consonance, mainly on 'n' sounds, binds the four short lines of this stanza tightly together, working alongside rhyme and alliteration ('dance', 'drink', and 'blind', 'brush'). It also helps to create a lyrical, song-like feel, helping to depict carefree, musical subject of the lines.

**Another example …**
'After a Journey' by Thomas Hardy:

*Hereto I come to view a voiceless ghost;*
*Whither, O whither will its whim now draw me?*
*Up the cliff, down, till I'm lonely, lost,*
*And the unseen waters' ejaculations awe me.*
*Where you will next be there's no knowing …*

The abundant consonance on 'w' sounds helps to create a suitably ghostly atmosphere at the start of this text. Another example of ghostly 'w' consonance can be found in 'Shadwell Stair' by Wilfred Owen.

# Contraction

See: Elision

# Contrast

**What is it?**
Where a poem puts opposites (usually imagery) next to one another.

**What effect does it usually have?**
Contrast makes poems more vivid and striking.

**What else should I look out for?**
Very often contrast involves sensory imagery involving light and dark, hot and cold, loud and soft, etc. Contrast is often used in descriptions of the natural world and other settings.

**An example of how it works …**
'During Wind and Rain' by Thomas Hardy:

> *They are blithely breakfasting all—*
> *Men and maidens—yea,*
> *Under the summer tree,*
> *With a glimpse of the bay*
> *… Ah, no; the years O!*
> *And the rotten rose is ript from the wall*

Each stanza of this poem sets up a contrast between happy summer days of the past and the stormy weather of a melancholy present. Here the alliteration in the final line adds further emphasis to the shocking image of decay and malignant natural forces.

**Another example …**
'The School Boy' by William Blake:

> *I love to rise in a summer morn,*
> *When the birds sing on every tree;*
> *The distant huntsman winds his horn,*

*And the skylark sings with me …*

*But to go to school in a summer morn,—*
*O! It drives all joy away!*
*Under a cruel eye outworn,*
*The little ones spend the day*
*In sighing and dismay*

Here the poet creates a vivid contrast between the natural joys of childhood and the unnatural misery of confinement in the classroom.

# Dash

**What is it?**
A horizontal line in a sentence that is longer than a hyphen.

**What effect does it usually have?**
Dashes tend to convey a sense of energy or spontaneity; in different situations they can also be used (like the ellipsis) to add a pause or silence, conveying the idea that the speaker has trailed off, lost in thought, or (in dialogue) that the speaker has been interrupted.

**What else should I look out for?**
Faltering speech and breathless excitement is effectively conveyed using dashes. They are also used to create a more speech-like, informal style, and may be used as a relaxed alternative to other punctuation (especially the colon, or the pair of commas around a subclause).

**An example of how it works …**
'Ode to a Nightingale' by John Keats:

> *Was it a vision, or a waking dream?*
> *Fled is that music:—Do I wake or sleep?*

The dash in the last line of the poem helps to convey the poet's sense of bewilderment as he emerges from the reverie of his poetic vision.

**Another example …**
'The Secret' by Emily Dickinson:

> *The skies can't keep their secret!*
> *They tell it to the hills—*
> *The hills just tell the orchards—*
> *And they the daffodils!*

The dashes used here are used as a more energetic alternative to commas, conveying the speaker's joyous response to the 'new-fashioned world' after the snows have melted.

# Diacope

**What is it?**
A type of repetition where a word is repeated with other words in between; this is usually just called **repetition** unless there is a need to distinguish it from other types (e.g. epizeuxis).

**What effect does it usually have?**
Diacope raises the importance of the repeated word, emphasising both its meaning and the sound of the word to create a musical effect.

**What else should I look out for?**
Repetition can create a feeling of insistence or obsession, which affects the tone of the text. Often there is an alternative to repeating the same word. To hear the effect of the diacope, try replacing the second or third use of the word with a different word with the same meaning.

**An example of how it works …**
'The Send-Off' by Wilfred Owen:

> *A few, a few, too few for drums and yells,*
> *May creep back, silent*

The fact that so 'few' men will return from the war is stressed by the use of diacope at the start of the line.

**Another example …**
'Sonnet 65' by William Shakespeare:

> *Where …*
> *Shall Time's best jewel from Time's chest lie hid?*

The frequent repetition of 'Time', here and elsewhere in the Sonnets, creates a sense of obsession; the speaker wrestles with the power of time again and again, portraying an endless war between time and beauty.

# Dialect

**What is it?**
The use of words or phrases in non-standard English, or the imitation of different accents. Also called **vernacular poetry**.

**What effect does it usually have?**
Enabling the reader to hear the way a character actually speaks tends to bring them closer. Dialect also makes poems seem more authentic or realistic and helps to establish a strong sense of place.

**What else should I look out for?**
Because the language of poetry has traditionally been considered superior to everyday speech, including dialect can suggest irreverence, or a rejection of the snobbery sometimes associated with literature. It also implies that the poet values the type of person being portrayed, and believes their form of English is equally valid and worth honouring in the poetic form.

**An example of how it works …**
'Homesick Blues' by Langston Hughes:

> *De railroad bridge's*
> *A sad song in de air.*
> *Ever time de trains pass*
> *I wants to go somewhere*

Here the poet reproduced the speech of a black American longing to return home to the South. The use of dialect makes the poem resemble a blues song, and makes us sympathise more strongly with the speaker.

# Dissonance

**What is it?**
Use of words that sound deliberately harsh and inharmonious together.

**What effect does it usually have?**
Dissonance creates a jarring, ugly effect, helping the poet to convey disgust, anger or discomfort.

**What else should I look out for?**
In order to accentuate shock or another type of impact, **dissonant** phrases often come after a passage of mellifluous effect. Dissonance is usually the result of packing a line with plosive consonants, with short vowels; the verse is usually irregular, with spondees and awkward enjambment.

**An example of how it works …**
'The Sentry' by Wilfred Owen:

> *Eyeballs, huge-balled like squids',*
> *Watch my dreams still*

The speaker conveys his horror at remembering a soldier blinded in an explosion. The ugly combination of plosives and sibilants, the spondaic 'huge-balled', and the awkward repetition of 'ball', and the grotesque simile, make these lines uniquely disturbing.

**Another example …**
'Sonnet 65' by William Shakespeare:

> *O, how shall summer's honey breath hold out*
> *Against the wrackful siege of battering days…*

The poet's dismay at the destruction caused by time, expressed in terms of war-imagery, is reinforced by the combination of harsh plosives and short vowels in the second line (especially in 'wrackful' and 'battering'). This contrasts greatly with the softness of the preceding line, with its honey imagery, assonance, and soft nasals, fricatives and aspirants ('summer', 'honey', 'hold'), which help portray the wonderful beauty of summer and youth.

# Dissonantal Rhyme

See: Pararhyme

# Double Rhyme

**What is it?**
Where words rhyme on two syllables rather than one, and the second syllable is stressed (see Understanding Versification). Some use the term to refer to feminine rhyme.

**What effect does it usually have?**
Rhymes connect words together in order to reinforce meaning, or to make a contrast. Rhyming always emphasises words, but the second word of the rhyming pair, called the clinching word, carries more emphasis than the first.

**What else should I look out for?**
Double rhymes often have an impact on tone and atmosphere, giving poems a jaunty, witty, or humorous quality.

**An example of how it works …**
'Nothing Gold Can Stay' by Robert Frost:

> *Then leaf subsides to leaf.*
> *So Eden sank to grief*

Here double rhyme occurs at the poem's crucial point: after describing the beauty of spring leaves in the simplest of terms, the poet unexpectedly alludes to the original sin. The vertiginous way this line suddenly deepens the poem is compounded by the linking of 'leaf' with the seriousness of 'grief' (the clinching word of the double rhyme). Since the speaker is now preoccupied with mankind's fallen condition, it has become a moral poem as well as a reflection on mutability and the nature of beauty.

**Another example …**

Don Juan, Canto I by Lord Byron:

> *In every Christian language ev<u>er named</u> …*
> *She made the cleverest people quite <u>ashamed</u>.*

The double rhyme in this line from near the start of the work helps to establish both the irreverent, light-hearted mood of the poem, and the playfulness that will become typical of the narrator's treatment of his characters.

# Dysphemism

**What is it?**
Using words that are deliberately blunt, offensive, or direct;
the opposite of euphemism.

**What effect does it usually have?**
Dysphemism usually shocks the reader. It often serves to
present the speaker as insensitive or unsympathetic.

**What else should I look out for?**
Sometimes dysphemism can be used for humorous effect.

**An example of how it works …**
'The Sentry' by Wilfred Owen:

> *Those other wretches, how they bled and spewed*

Here the dysphemistic language helps to convey how the
officer describing the conditions in the trenches has become
desensitised by constant exposure to the horrors of war.

**Another example …**
'The Miller's Tale' by Geoffrey Chaucer:

> *This Nicholas anon let flee a fart,*
> *As great as it had been a thunder-dent*

As we approach the climax of this tale, the dysphemistic
language has a comic effect, enhanced by the mischievous
verb choice 'flee', and the thunder-clap simile in the
following line.

# Elision

### What is it?
Where a word is shortened by removing letters mid-word, as in o'er (over), ne'er (never), e'en (even), or hea'en (heaven); as elision is a type of **contraction**, the missing letter or letters are indicated with an apostrophe. Also called **syncope**.

### What effect does it usually have?
Elision makes the verse more concentrated; it has a similar effect to ellipsis. Poets normally use syncope to help them fit words to a line of verse.

### What else should I look out for?
Because words like o'er are conventional poeticisms, they are sometimes used to create make a poem sound more traditional, or to resemble hymns, or classic poetry of a bygone age.

### An example of how it works …
'Sonnet 12' by William Shakespeare:

> *And sable curls all silvered o'er with white*

Here Shakespeare **elides** the 'v' reducing the word 'over' one syllable, thus forming a perfectly regular line of iambic pentameter; this has the effect of recalling the ticking clock of the poem's opening line – a reminder that time never for a moment stands still.

# Ellipsis

**What is it?**
The removal of one or more of the less important words from a phrase to shorten it.

**What effect does it usually have?**
Ellipsis creates a sense of compression or concentration, since the 'spacer' words brings the operative words of a phrase closer together; this makes the text feel denser and heightens its emotional intensity.

**What else should I look out for?**
The concision caused by ellipsis can give lines a memorable, epigrammatic power. Ellipsis very often also leads to ambiguity. When thinking about the effect, try adding the words back in and comparing the two versions

**An example of how it works …**
*Don Juan*, Canto II by Lord Byron:

> *man, to man so oft unjust,*
> *Is always so to women; one sole bond*
> *Awaits them, treachery is all their trust*

Here the author considers the plight of women, doomed to be bound in marriage to a faithless husband. The last line does not mean (as it appears) that their trust is treacherous, but that 'treachery is all [they are given in return for] their trust'. The use of ellipsis makes the line feel blunt and cold, which suits the bitter tone of the stanza.

**Another example …**
'The Fly' by William Blake:

*If thought is life*
*And strength and breath,*
*And the want*
*Of thought is death,*

*Then am I*
*A happy fly*

The **elliptical** phrasing in these lines renders the second line—and therefore the whole poem—highly ambiguous. Is Blake's main subject 'life' or 'thought'? Does he mean that 'life' consists of no more than 'thought' and the 'strength' and 'breath' of the physical body? Or is he saying that 'life', 'strength' and 'breath' exist only in 'thought'? Such ambiguities give the poem an enigmatic quality that make it endlessly fascinating.

# Ellipsis (Punctuation)

**What is it?**
Three dots in row (…); after a full stop, four dots.

**What effect does it usually have?**
Like dashes, **ellipses** adds pauses or silences, conveying the idea that the speaker has trailed off, lost in thought. They often create a wistful, melancholic atmosphere.

**What else should I look out for?**
Used in essays to indicate that some of a quoted text has been cut out, in poems ellipsis also suggest that something is missing or not being expressed; it can portray the speaker as overwhelmed and therefore unable to express themselves fluently, or unable to find adequate words for what they are experiencing.

**An example of how it works …**
'Sea Song' by Katherine Mansfield:

> *I am old. I'm too cold.*
> *I am frightened … the sea*
> *Is too loud … it is lost,*
> *It is gone …*

Here the use of ellipsis slows the pace as we approach the last lines of the poem, creating a sinister air of mystery.

# End Stop

See: Enjambment

# Enjambment

**What is it?**
Where a line runs straight onto the next without pausing (i.e. when it is **enjambed** rather than being **end-stopped** using a punctuation mark). Stanzas may be enjambed as well as individual lines.

**What effect does it usually have?**
Enjambment creates a sense of energy, urgency and movement, as the sense rushes on, as if it cannot be contained within the line; it usually increases the pace.

**What else should I look out for?**
Because we expect most lines of poetry to be end-stopped, enjambment can create a surprise; it tends to be used (along with other features of irregular verse) at times of excitement or to indicate a sense of disorder – e.g. describing a storm – or passion and freedom.

**An example of how it works …**
*The Prelude* by William Wordsworth:

> *I wheeled about*
> *Proud and exulting, like an untired horse*
> *That cares not for its home. All shod with steel*
> *We hissed along the polished ice in games*
> *Confederate, imitative of the chase*
> *And woodland pleasures*

Here Wordsworth evokes the joyful sports of his childhood, ice-skating and chasing his friends. The enjambment of all six lines creates a sense of headlong rushing from one game to the next, speed, and excitement; sibilance is used to re-create the sound of skating (shod, steel, hissed, polished, ice games).

# Enumeration

**What is it?**
Using lists.

**What effect does it usually have?**
Enumeration makes quite simple sentence structures, long or short, which often speeds up the pace.

**What else should I look out for?**
The last item in the list tends to carry the most emphasis; enumeration can create a sense of building towards an emotional climax. Many poems begin with a description of setting involving the use of enumeration.

**An example of how it works …**
'Stanzas Written in Dejection, near Naples' by P. B. Shelley:

> *The sun is warm, the sky is clear,*
> *The waves are dancing fast and bright,*
> *Blue isles and snowy mountains wear*
> *The purple noon's transparent might,*
> *The breath of the moist earth is light,*
> *Around its unexpanded buds*

Here the poet enumerates his various impressions of the Italian landscape to create a striking opening for this poem and establish a positive atmosphere, soon to be snatched away since the speaker lacks the 'hope' and 'health' needed to enjoy them.

# Epic Simile

See: Extended Simile

# Epizeuxis

**What is it?**
The repetition of a word with no other words in between.

**What effect does it usually have?**
Epizeuxis creates an emotional or dramatic climax. As with other forms of repetition, it may also have a musical effect.

**What else should I look out for?**
Epizeuxis has a simplicity that communicates very directly, on a deep level. When King Lear carries the body of his murdered daughter onto the stage, in one of the most powerful moments in all theatre, Shakespeare gives him a line of epizeuxis before he dies of grief: 'Never, never, never, never, never'.

**An example of how it works …**
'The Last Laugh' by Wilfred Owen:

> *Another sighed—'O Mother,—Mother,—Dad!'*
> *Then smiled at nothing*

In this poignant depiction of a wounded soldier's last moments, the epizeuxis has a powerful dramatic impact in contrast to the cold, blunt line that follows.

**Another example …**
'Canto IV' by Ezra Pound:

> *Diana,*
> *Nymphs, white-gathered about her, and the air, air,*
> *Shaking, air alight with the goddess*
> *            fanning their hair in the dark,*
> *Lifting, lifting and waffing*

The repetition of the words 'air' and 'lifting' helps create a sense of breathless rapture at the sight of Diana and her nymphs drying their hair in golden light, mimicking Actaeon's imminent reaction. Epizeuxis works with assonance and consonance to enhance the lyrical beauty of the lines.

# Euphemism

**What is it?**
Using a delicate, inoffensive, or indirect word or phrase (e.g. passed) rather than a more blunt or direct one (e.g. died).

**What effect does it usually have?**
In poetry, euphemisms normally enable the writer to refer to matters that might otherwise be considered rude or inappropriate (especially those of a sexual nature, or to do with bodily functions).

**What else should I look out for?**
Euphemistic language often involves imagery that can be worth analysing. Some euphemisms are amusing, or may help to colour our view of the speaker in another way.

**An example of how it works …**
'Isabella' by John Keats:

> *Those dainties made to still an infant's cries*

This delicate way of referring to Isabella's breasts is in keeping with the medieval style and subject matter of the poem. The line also serves to remind us of the future of motherhood that has been cruelly snatched from her by the murder of her beloved.

# Eye Rhyme

**What is it?**
Where line-end words are rhymed with words of similar spelling, giving the appearance, but not the sound, of rhyme (e.g. 'daughter … laughter'). Some examples from older texts appear to be eye rhymes, but are actually **historic rhymes**.

**What effect does it usually have?**
Rhymes connect words together in order to reinforce meaning, or to make a contrast. Rhyming always emphasises words, but the second word of the rhyming pair, called the clinching word, carries more emphasis than the first.

**What else should I look out for?**
Like half-rhyme and pararhyme, eye rhyme tends to be used where full rhyming is considered too euphonious, too conspicuous, too conventional, or too obvious.

**An example of how it works …**
'Futility' by Wilfred Owen:

> *If anything might rouse him <u>now</u>*
> *The kind old sun will <u>know</u>*

Here the eye rhyme creates a sense of mismatch, of something not quite right. This suits the subject of the poem: the speaker can hardly believe that his fallen comrade, who appears just to be sleeping, has died of his wounds.

# Exclamation Mark

**What is it?**

A punctuation mark (!) that usually stands in for a full stop.

**What effect does it usually have?**

Exclamation marks indicate rising volume or pitch; usually they involve a sense of comedy, extremes of emotion, or serve to emphasise a phrase.

**What else should I look out for?**

Disorder, a lack of control or composure often accompanies exclamation marks, so they tend to be found alongside irregular verse features; they also help to create a sense of climax in longer poems.

**An example of how it works …**

'Wild Nights!' by Emily Dickinson:

> *Wild Nights—Wild Nights!*
> *Were I with thee*
> *Wild Nights should be*
> *Our luxury!*

In this passionate lyric, the longing of the speaker is conveyed in a series of exclamations; the use of enjambment, dashes, and irregular verse also contribute to the impression that her desires are boiling over, too strong to be restrained.

**Another example …**

'Ode to the West Wind' by P. B. Shelley:

> *Oh, lift me as a wave, a leaf, a cloud!*
> *I fall upon the thorns of life! I bleed!*

The exclamations work together with the rapid monosyllables, and the interjection and asyndetic list in the first line, to help raise the emotions of this poem to fever pitch, whilst the poet is consumed by his vision of the West Wind's awesome power.

# Extended Simile

**What is it?**
Where a simile is extended over a number of lines; when an extended similes in a narrative poem is long enough to become a digression, it is called an **epic simile**.

**What effect does it usually have?**
Similes enable poets to bring imagery into the poem, giving the text greater impact and emotional power.

**What else should I look out for?**
Whereas we might use quick similes in life to explain things more clearly (e.g. a parsnip is like a carrot) extended similes often make a poem richer and more ambiguous.

**An example of how it works …**
'Sonnet 33' by William Shakespeare:

> *Even so my sun one early morn did shine*
> *With all-triumphant splendour on my brow;*
> *But out, alack! he was but one hour mine;*
> *The region cloud hath masked him from me now*

These four lines are from a poem exploring a simile comparing the sun being masked by clouds with the beloved's beauty being hidden from the poet. It is unclear whether the beloved is absent, has been unfaithful, or has stopped showing affection to the poet – the poem can support all three, and indeed more, interpretations, because of the way that the imagery is described.

# Feminine Line Ending

### What is it?
Where a line of iambic verse ends with an additional, unstressed syllable; also called just a **feminine ending**. See Understanding Versification.

### What effect does it usually have?
Feminine line endings elongate the line, and usually create a relatively looser, more relaxed feel to the verse.

### What else should I look out for?
Where feminine line endings occur alongside other irregular features, then the result is a greater sense of disorder. Some poets use lines with feminine endings when describing female or feminine subjects, punning on the term (which has been used since Elizabethan times).

### An example of how it works ...
'Ode to the West Wind' by P. B. Shelley:

> *O wild West Wind, thou breath of Autumn's being,*
> *Thou, from whose unseen presence the leaves dead*
> *Are driven, like ghosts from an enchanter fleeing,*
> *Yellow, and black, and pale, and hectic red ...*

This poem opens with a wild burst of energy, mimicking the action of the wind being invoked, as it sweeps away the leaves of the old year to make way for fresh growth in the new. The feminine line endings 'being' and 'fleeing' lengthen the first and third lines beyond the expected ten syllables, and work alongside other irregular features (the enjambment on the second line, the caesuras in the first and third lines, the spondaic 'leaves dead') to create a sense that the power of the wind cannot be constrained.

**Another example …**

'Sonnet 20' by William Shakespeare:

> *A woman's face with nature's own hand painted*
> *Hast thou, the master-mistress of my passion*

Here Shakespeare opens the poem as he will continue in every line to the end, playfully using feminine line endings. Since the poem entirely concerns the young man's feminine qualities, this contributes towards the poem's light-hearted, witty character.

# Feminine Rhyme

**What is it?**
Where words rhyme on two syllables rather than one, and
the second syllable is unstressed (see Understanding
Versification).

**What effect does it usually have?**
Rhymes connect words together in order to reinforce
meaning, or to make a contrast. Rhyming always emphasises
words, but the second word of the rhyming pair, called the
clinching word, carries more emphasis than the first.

**What else should I look out for?**
Like double rhymes, feminine rhymes often have an impact
on tone and atmosphere, giving poems a light-hearted,
humorous quality. Line-endings with an unstressed final
syllable have been called 'feminine' since the fourteenth
century (because of feminine adjectives in Occitan, the
language of the troubadour poets); some poets therefore play
on the association when portraying females or feminine
qualities.

**An example of how it works …**
'We Talked with Each Other' by Emily Dickinson:

> *We were listening to the seconds' <u>Races</u>*
> *And the Hoofs of the Clock—*
> *Pausing in Front of our Palsied <u>Faces</u>*
> *Time compassion took—*

Here the poet uses feminine rhyme to stress the young
couple's horror ('palsied faces') at the rapid passage of time
('races'), connecting the words and giving both a special
resonance in the text.

**Another example …**
'Sonnet 20' by William Shakespeare:

*A woman's face with nature's own hand painted*
*Hast thou, the master-mistress of my passion;*
*A woman's gentle heart, but not acquainted*
*With shifting change as is false women's fashion*

Shakespeare playfully gave each of the fourteen lines of this poem a feminine rhyme, helping to portray the femininity of the young man he is addressing.

# Forced Rhyme

### What is it?
Where a word is made to rhyme by straining the language in some way, usually by bending the rules of grammar or pronunciation.

### What effect does it usually have?
Forced rhymes usually have a playful, comic effect; they tend to imply that the poet is struggling, rushing, or incompetent. Some writers, such as Ogden Nash, have used forced rhymes deliberately to create a form of doggerel for popular entertainment.

### What else should I look out for?
Like half-rhymes, forced rhymes tend to jar, since the clinching word fails to match the preceding one of the pair, of fails to comply with the rhyme scheme. This feeling may be exploited for different effects.

### An example of how it works …
*Don Juan*, Canto II by Lord Byron:

> *And though 'tis true that Man can only <u>die once</u>,*
> *'Tis not so pleasant in the Gulph of <u>Lyons</u>*

These lines, from the end of a stanza describing how the sailors pass a sail under the keel, strike a discordant note. Although we are expecting a rhyming couplet the last word of the poem fails, just as the sailors' desperate, and rather pathetic attempts to stop the ship from sinking also fail.

# Fourteener

See: Long Line

# Frame Rhyme

See: Pararhyme

# Fricatives

**What is it?**
Using a number of words close together containing fricative consonants (*f, v, th* sounds). See Describing Sound in Poetry.

**What effect does it usually have?**
Fricatives are often used onomatopoeically to represent wind, especially the noise of wind in trees or at sea (which is called 'soughing', itself an onomatopoeic word containing a fricative); or to represent breathing. Settings described using many fricatives tend to be soft ('feathery'), warm and inviting.

**What else should I look out for?**
The abundance of fricatives can create resonant, memorable phrases, as with the proverb 'Fortune favours the brave' (Virgil), which contains fricative alliteration, consonance *and* assonance.

**An example of how it works …**
'The Rime of the Ancient Mariner' by Samuel Taylor Coleridge:

> *The fair breeze blew, the white foam flew,*
> *The furrow followed free*

Here fricative alliteration mimics the sound of wind on the waves and the ship cutting a path through the ocean.

# Gerund

See: Present Participles

# Guttural

**What is it?**
Using a number of words close together containing gutturals, the hardest type of plosive consonant (k and g sounds). See Describing Sound in Poetry.

**What effect does it usually have?**
Gutturals lend texts a tough, harsh sound. Like the other plosives, they can help to convey anger, especially during dialogue.

**What else should I look out for?**
Some poets choose words containing many clusters of guttural sounds to make their English sound closer to Anglo Saxon, Gaelic or certain regional accents or dialects (e.g. Ted Hughes and Seamus Heaney).

**An example of how it works ...**
'The Sentry' by Wilfred Owen:

> *Rain ... choked the steps too thick with clay to climb*
> *What murk or air remained stank old*

The poet here conveys both the harsh conditions in the trenches and his anger and disgust, choosing a number of words containing gutturals: 'choke', 'think', 'clay', 'climb', 'murk', and 'stank'.

# Half-Rhyme

**What is it?**
Where two words almost, but do not fully, rhyme. Usually, the vowel matches and the consonant differs slightly ('face … waste') or where the consonant matches, but the vowel differs ('race … farce'). Also called **slant rhyme**, **near rhyme**, and **semi-rhyme**.

**What effect does it usually have?**
Rhymes connect words together in order to reinforce meaning, or to make a contrast. Rhyming always emphasises words, but the second word of the rhyming pair, called the clinching word, carries more emphasis than the first.

**What else should I look out for?**
Like pararhyme and eye rhyme, half-rhyme tends to be used where full rhyming is considered too euphonious, too conspicuous, too conventional, or too obvious. Some examples appear to be half-rhyme but are actually historic rhyme (e.g. 'stone' and 'frown' in Shelley's 'Ozymandias').

**An example of how it works …**
'Spring' by William Blake:

> *Little boy,*
> *Full of joy;*
> *Little girl,*
> *Sweet and small;*
> *Cock does crow,*
> *So do you;*
> *Merry voice,*
> *Infant noise*

In this poem Blake uses both full rhyme ('boy ... joy') and a string of half-rhymes which suit the rough-hewn quality of the poem, helping to lend it a vigorous, rustic quality. The half-rhymes work closely in these short lines with sibilance and alliteration, to create a parallel between the children's cries and the calls of surrounding animals.

### Another example ...

'The Pardoner's Tale' by Geoffrey Chaucer:

> *As shameful deeth as herte may devise*
> *Come to thise juges and hire advocats!*
> *Algate this sely mayde is slayn, allas!*

Here the use of half-rhyme on a pair of exclamations and an interjection helps to convey the anger of the Host, who is beside himself because of the shocking abuse suffered by the good Virginia in the preceding tale of the sequence, told by the Physician.

# Heroic Couplet

See: Rhyming Couplet

# Historic Rhyme

### What is it?
Where two words, which would have rhymed fully in the poet's time, now take on the appearance of an eye rhyme, due to changes that have occurred in the pronunciation of English. Shakespeare frequently rhymes 'love' with 'move' and 'prove'; these have now become historic rhymes.

### What effect does it usually have?
Historic rhymes are best treated as having the same effect as full rhymes.

### What else should I look out for?
Some poets have used historic rhymes anachronistically to evoke poetry of the distant past (e.g. W. H. Auden in 'We must lose our <u>loves</u>, On each beast and bird that <u>moves</u>.')

### An example of how it works …
'Sonnet 26' by William Shakespeare:

> *Then happy I, that love and am <u>beloved</u>,*
> *Where I may not remove nor be <u>removed</u>*

In this example, the rhymes at end-line would originally have complemented the internal rhymes formed by the polyptoton ('love … beloved', 'remove … removed') creating a rich pattern of harmony befitting the final couplet of this love poem.

# Hypallage

See: Transferred Epithet

# Hyperbaton

**What is it?**
Where the word order has been significantly changed from English norms.

**What effect does it usually have?**
Hyperbaton is one of the methods by which poets elevate their language above everyday speech. As it is used so often to position words at the end of lines for rhyming, it tends to be so common that it is only worth commenting upon when it renders a phrase particularly eloquent, striking or memorable.

**What else should I look out for?**
Sometimes hyperbaton is used to create a sense of the new, the strange, or the wonderful; other poets, such as Milton, frequently uses a word order that sounds more Latin than English, to evoke the grandeur of ancient epics (e.g. by positioning adjectives after the noun, 'A Dungeon horrible').

**An example of how it works …**
'I Am the Ghost of Shadwell Stair' by Wilfred Owen:

> *From the banks*
> *Dolorously the shipping clanks*

The hyperbaton of these lines contributes to the strange atmosphere being described ('the shipping clanks dolorously from the banks' would be the usual word order in English). The onomatopoeic word 'clanks', which calls to mind ghostly rattling chains, is given particular weight by its position at the end of the second line, clinching a rhyming couplet.

# Hyperbole

**What is it?**
An overstatement or exaggeration made for poetic effect.

**What effect does it usually have?**
Hyperboles are usually employed to emphasise a point, to make imagery more striking, or for dramatic impact.

**What else should I look out for?**
Very often hyperbole is used to convey the intensity of emotion (especially love), for the sake of flattery, or to enhance the setting of a poem.

**An example of how it works …**
'Upon his Saddle' by Emily Dickinson:

> *a Bird …*
> *crossed a thousand Trees*
> *.. lifted up his Throat*
> *And squandered such a Note*
> *A Universe that overheard*
> *Is stricken by it yet*

In this short lyric, the 'thousand' trees and the idea of a listening 'universe' are **hyperboles** serving to convey the unsurpassed beauty of the bird's song.

**Another example …**
'Mental Cases' by Wilfred Owen:

> *what … Gouged these chasms round their fretted sockets?*

To describe the dark shadows around the eyes of war veterans as 'chasms' is clearly **hyperbolic**; the word helps to convey the speaker's horror at the sight of the men, as well as connecting with the other 'hellish' imagery of the poem.

# Hyphenation

**What is it?**
Where two (or more) words are joined together using
**hyphens** (horizontal lines that are shorter than dashes).

**What effect does it usually have?**
Hyphenation combines words to make a new one, creating a
sense that what is being described is itself new, rare or
unique.

**What else should I look out for?**
Where the first word is a monosyllable, hyphenation usually
results in a spondee, helping to emphasise the word.

**An example of how it works …**
'Bare Fig Trees' by D. H. Lawrence:

> *Rather like an octopus,*
> > *but strange and sweet-myriad-limbed octopus;*
> *Like a nude, like a rock-living, sweet-fleshed sea-anemone,*
> *Flourishing from the rock*

The speaker conveys the astonishing beauty of the trees, and
their strange energy, in a series of outlandish similes, made
even more strange and intense by the use of hyphenation.

**Another example …**
'Afterwards' by Thomas Hardy:

> *The May month flaps its glad green leaves like wings,*
> *Delicate-filmed as new-spun silk*

The hyphenation of the images in the second line helps to convey their freshness, and with 'new spun' forming a further spondee – on top of the two molossi of the first line – to create an awkward feeling that fits the restless mood of the poem.

# Imagery

### What is it?
The visual and other sense-impressions made by the text, especially those created by the use of metaphor and simile.

### What effect does it usually have?
Imagery enables the reader to experience ideas or emotions for themselves, to 'see' them in the imagination, and very often to hear or feel them too, bringing us closer to the speaker.

### What else should I look out for?
As well as communicating thought and feeling, patterns of imagery can help to establish tone, or may present the speaker in a particular way. Poets often choose images that contribute towards the setting of the poem, even when mainly concerned with describing other subjects.

### An example of how it works …
'Sonnet 2' by William Shakespeare:

> *When forty winters shall besiege thy brow*
> *And dig deep trenches in thy beauty's field*

Here the imagery of war ('besiege', 'trenches', 'field') is used to describe the impact time will have upon the face ('brow') of the beloved. The disturbing violence of the metaphor makes an arresting opening for this poem, contrasting with the far gentler flower imagery of the preceding poem in the set.

# Imperative

**What is it?**
Giving a command.

**What effect does it usually have?**
Using the imperative, like asking questions, is a way to engage the reader directly in the text.

**What else should I look out for?**
The imperative can imply a certain power relationship, where the speaker positions him or herself above the reader.

**An example of how it works …**
'Ode to the West Wind' by P. B. Shelley:

> *Be thou, Spirit fierce,*
> *My spirit! Be thou me, impetuous one!*

At the climax of the poem, Shelley tells the West Wind to enter him so that he can share in its power.

**Another example …**
'The Little Boy Lost' by William Blake:

> *Oh do not walk so fast.*
> *Speak father, speak to your little boy*

Here the imperative lends dramatic emphasis to the need for the father (i.e. God) to talk to the boy, to prevent him from losing his way and falling into sin.

# Interjection

**What is it?**
A word or short phrase added to a sentence to express an emotional reaction; usually an exclamation (e.g. ah! oh!)

**What effect does it usually have?**
Interjections convey the idea that the speaker is so overwhelmed by what they are saying that they interrupt themselves; they heighten the emotional impact of a poem and lend variety. They act as signals indicating how the reader is expected to react.

**What else should I look out for?**
Because interjections are often abrupt, they often create surprise (the word 'interjection' literally means something 'thrown' in). They also make the tone of the poem livelier and more spontaneous. Apostrophes are often accompanied by interjections and, like apostrophes, they may be used to give poems an engaging opening.

**An example of how it works ...**
'Time and Eternity, V' by Emily Dickinson:

> *Alas! how heedless were the eyes*
> *On whom the summer shone!*

Here the poet is describing birds happy in their nests; the interjection creates a sense of sympathy for the creatures, who are oblivious to the threat of the storm that lies in wait.

**Another example ...**
'Death of Do Dirty' by Langston Hughes:

> *An' de ones that kilt him,—*
> *Damn their souls,—*

> *I'm gonna fill 'em up full o'*
> *Bullet holes.*

The phrase that is **interjected** here conveys the speaker's determination to avenge himself on the killers, which brings the poem to a climax before it ends.

# Internal Rhyme

### What is it?
Where words are rhymed with others within, rather than at the end of lines.

### What effect does it usually have?
Rhymes connect words together in order to reinforce meaning, or to make a contrast. Rhyming always emphasises words, but the second word of the rhyming pair, called the clinching word, carries more emphasis than the first.

### What else should I look out for?
Internal rhymes, when they are plentiful, create a sense of harmony, or words being well-chosen and belonging together. Where internal half-rhymes are used, the distinction begins to blur between rhyming and consonance or assonance.

### An example of how it works ...
'Mental Cases' by Wilfred Owen:

> *Batter of guns and shatter of flying muscles,*
> *Carnage incomparable*

Here the use of internal rhyme gives the shocking visual imagery of these lines an additional aural quality, helping to stress the onomatopoeic 'batter' and 'shatter'.

# Listing

See: Enumeration

# Long Line

**What is it?**
A line significantly longer than neighbouring lines; a line of twelve syllables or more.

**What effect does it usually have?**
Long lines tend to slow the pace; when used one after another, they make poems feel denser, heavier, more serious than shorter lines, especially when in block form.

**What else should I look out for?**
A twelve-syllable line of iambic hexameter is called an **alexandrine**; iambic heptameters are called **fourteeners** and are associated with ballads and folk songs. Beware of long lines that have been wrapped to fit the margins of the printed page – this is usually a decision made by the publisher, rather than the poet.

**An example of how it works …**
'Afterwards' by Thomas Hardy:

> *If I pass during some nocturnal blackness, mothy and warm,*
> *When the hedgehog travels furtively over the lawn*

Here the use of long lines help to create a suitably sombre, melancholy tone, as the elderly poet pictures the moment of his death.

# Long Vowels

**What is it?**
Using many words containing long vowel sounds, especially **open vowels** (not followed by a consonant).

**What effect does it usually have?**
Long vowels tend to slow the pace, creating a languorous or lethargic mood.

**What else should I look out for?**
Often long vowels are used when the poet is enjoying describing a beautiful setting, relishing an experience, or when there is a sense of longing or nostalgia; they are also found to reflect the poet's low spirits, or a sense of stasis or entrapment.

**An example of how it works …**
'Stanzas Written in Dejection, near Naples' by P. B. Shelley:

> I could lie down like a tired child,
> And weep away the life of care
> Which I have borne and yet must bear,
> Till death like sleep might steal on me,
> And I might feel in the warm air
> My cheek grow cold, and hear the sea
> Breathe o'er my dying brain its last monotony

The numerous long vowels in these lines ('weep', 'borne', 'steal', 'feel', 'warm'), together with the open vowels in the rhyming end-words ('care', 'bear', 'air', 'sea', 'me') suit the melancholic, enervated mood of the poem, written when Shelley was in the depths of depression.

# Masculine Rhyme

See: Rhyme

# Metaphor

### What is it?
Where a poem refers to one thing by means of another (e.g. saying a beautiful woman 'is' a rose; or love 'is' a thunderbolt). Metaphors can be implied rather than stated directly (e.g. saying a woman pricked you with her thorns, which *implies* that she is a rose; or saying that love struck with a blinding flash out of nowhere).

### What effect does it usually have?
Metaphor enables the poet to bring imagery into the text to visualise ideas or feelings; the **metaphorical** nature or poetic language is arguably its most important feature, since it renders it more so much more colourful, vivid and ambiguous than everyday speech.

### What else should I look out for?
As well as interrogating individual metaphors—asking yourself what they imply about the ideas and feelings being communicated, and the speaker's imagination or state of mind—it is worth analysing the patterns of imagery produced by metaphor, and how metaphor brings ideas or different things in combination with one another.

### An example of how it works ...
'Sonnet 2' by William Shakespeare:

> *When forty winters shall besiege thy brow*
> *And dig deep trenches in thy beauty's field*

Here the poet implies that time is 'attacking' the beautiful face ('brow') of his beloved by using the diction of war ('besiege', 'trenches', 'field'). The disturbing violence of the metaphor makes an arresting opening for this poem, contrasting with the far gentler flower metaphors of the preceding poem in the set. It also positions the speaker as one who may 'defend' the beloved, and save him by preserving their beauty forever in his timeless art.

**Another example …**
'Sonnet 19' by William Shakespeare:

> *carve not with thy hours my love's fair brow,*
> *Nor draw no lines there with thine antique pen*

Here the poet begs time not to change the youthful beauty of his beloved's face. The verbs 'carving' and 'drawing' imply that time is a sort of artist; he begs time to leave the beloved as a 'pattern' (a human model, for artists to copy) so that people in future can measure their own looks against true perfection.

# Metonymy

### What is it?
Where a word is swapped for another closely related to it;
e.g. in the phrase 'a tasty dish', where 'dish' replaces 'meal'.

### What effect does it usually have?
In poetry, metonymy enables the poet to include imagery
instead of more predicable words, enlivening and freshening
the language.

### What else should I look out for?
Although we use metonymy in everyday speech without
causing any confusion (in the example above, it is easy to
understand that it is the food, not the plate, that tastes good!)
in poetry metonymy may create ambiguity; it can sometimes
be unclear whether a poet intends words or phrases to be
understood literally or **metonymically**.

### An example of how it works …
'Ode to a Nightingale' by John Keats:

> *O for a beaker full of the warm South*

Here the poet longs for a glass of wine, but the metonymy
'warm south' evokes scenes that accord with the imagery of
the previous line: 'Dance, and Provençal song, and sunburnt
mirth'.

### Another example …
'Sonnet 35' by William Shakespeare:

> *loathsome canker lives in sweetest bud*

In the first sonnet, the youth is referred to as a 'bud', a promising young man; some critics read this line metonymically, implying that the youth conceals corruption – or worse – beneath a handsome appearance, making it impossible for us to be certain about how to interpret this poem.

# Molossus

**What is it?**
A bunch of three stresses, one after the other. See
Understanding Versification.

**What effect does it usually have?**
Molossi, like spondees, are used to emphasise important
words or images.

**What else should I look out for?**
Sometimes a molossus will seem to halt the movement of
the poem, as the rhythm seems to catch on the words.

**An example of how it works …**
'Mental Cases' by Wilfred Owen:

> *teeth that leer like skulls' teeth wicked*

Here the molossus on the last three words of this phrase
accentuates the horror of the poet's description of these
men; the skull simile makes the men seem to be tormented
souls in hell, as they re-live their experiences of the
battlefield on a permanent loop.

**Another example …**
'Sonnet 43' by William Shakespeare:

> *All days are nights to see till I see thee,*
> *And nights bright days when dreams do show thee me*

Here the poet equates the absence of the beloved with darkness, and dreams of the beloved's beauty with light. The repetition of 'days', 'nights', 'see' and 'thee' combine with the molossus at 'nights bright days' to create an awkward conclusion to this sonnet, mimicking his perturbed state of mind.

# Monosyllables

**What is it?**
Using all (or mainly) one-syllable words.

**What effect does it usually have?**
Lines that are **monosyllabic** often feel more
straightforward, plain, stark or direct, since the diction will
generally be simpler.

**What else should I look out for?**
Sometimes monosyllables can create a feeling of
awkwardness.  Pace is not usually affected by the number of
syllables per word (since we run words together when
reading), though monosyllables usually make lines look
longer.

**An example of how it works ...**
'The Send-Off' by Wilfred Owen:

> *Their breasts were stuck all white with wreath and spray*
> *As men's are, dead*

In this blunt two-line stanza, the poet describes local men
marching off to war, unaware that certain death awaits nearly
all of them. The monosyllables help create a cold tone, as
well as conveying the simple, inescapable truth of the
situation.

**Another example ...**
'Sonnet 43' by William Shakespeare:

> *All days are nights to see till I see thee,*
> *And nights bright days when dreams do show thee me.*

Here the poet equates the absence of the beloved with darkness, and dreams of the beloved's beauty with light. The repetition of 'days', 'nights', 'see' and 'thee' work together with monosyllabic diction to create an awkwardness that mimics the lover's confused mental state.

# Mosaic Rhyme

### What is it?
Where a set of short words are combined to rhyme with a longer word.

### What effect does it usually have?
Because mosaic rhymes are rare and comparatively difficult to write, they tend to occur in isolation; this gives them greater emphasis than the more common forms of rhyme. Like double and triple rhymes, mosaic rhymes may be used for comic effect, and tend to bring with them a sense of showmanship or ingenuity.

### What else should I look out for?
When reading a mosaic rhyme the hand of the poet becomes visible; they may therefore take on the qualities of a forced rhyme.

### An example of how it works …
*Don Juan*, Canto I by Lord Byron:

> *But—Oh! ye lords of ladies intellectual,*
> *Inform us truly, have they not hen-peck'd you all?*

The ingenious mosaic triple rhyme closes the stanza with a showy flourish as the narrator characteristically makes light of his theme: the unfortunate marriages made by women to men of inferior intelligence.

### Another example …
'The Parliament of Fowls' by Geoffrey Chaucer:

> *A gardyn saw I, ful of blosmy bowes,*
> *Upon a river, in a grene mede,*
> *Ther as swetnesse evermore y-now is*

Here the beauty and harmony of this idyll is enhanced by the richness of the mosaic triple rhyme, which works alongside the lyricism of assonance ('grene mede'), alliteration ('blosmy blowes') and sibilance in the third line.

# Names

See: Proper Nouns

# Nasals

### What is it?
Using a number of words close together containing nasal consonants (*m, n, -ing*).

### What effect does it usually have?
Since nasals sound long and soft, they help slow pace and create a pleasant atmosphere.

### What else should I look out for?
Nasals convey a languorous mood or sense of relish (we naturally say 'mmm' when tasting something good); they may be used to contrast with harder consonants in nearby lines.

### An example of how it works …
*The Prelude* by William Wordsworth:

> *A lonely scene more lonesome, among woods*
> *At noon, and mid the calm of summer nights*
> *When by the margin of the trembling lake*
> *Beneath the gloomy hills I homeward went*

Here the nasals are used alongside long vowels ('noon', 'calm', 'gloomy') to help convey the poet's nostalgia for the summer evenings of his youth; he does not seem to want the experience to end.

### Another example …
'The Last Laugh' by Wilfred Owen:

> *'My Love!' one moaned. Love-languid seemed his mood,*
> *Till slowly lowered, his whole face kissed the mud*

The poet uses nasals and long vowels to reflect the 'languid' mood of the dying soldier, as he calls out to his sweetheart on the battlefield, choosing verbs such as 'seemed' and 'moaned'; this contrasts with the following line, where he face-plants the mud, and short vowels are used ('kissed', 'mud') to convey the indignity of his death.

# Near Rhyme

See: Half-Rhyme

# Negatives

**What is it?**
The repeated use of words such as 'no', 'not, 'never' etc.

**What effect does it usually have?**
Piling up negatives often creates a sense of disapproval, anger, or despair.

**What else should I look out for?**
Saying what something is *not* can be more powerful and expressive than saying what it *is*; sometimes this implies that the thing being observed falls short of what it should be.

**An example of how it works …**
'Spring Offensive' by Wilfred Owen:

> *No alarms*
> *Of bugles, no high flags, no clamorous haste*

The anaphoric repetition of negatives clearly underlines what is missing from the scene: though the soldiers are about to charge at the enemy, there is an empty stillness on the battlefield.

# Neologism

See: Coinage

# Onomatopoeia

**What is it?**

The use of words that seem to sound like what they describe (e.g. ping).

**What effect does it usually have?**

Onomatopoeic words make description more vivid and effective, since the reader can 'hear' what is being described as well as 'seeing' it in the imagination.

**What else should I look out for?**

As well as the obvious examples, onomatopoeia can be subtle. It can play an important role in creating an effective setting or establishing atmosphere. In unrhyming poems, onomatopoeia (along with assonance, alliteration, etc.) enhances the musical qualities of the text.

**An example of how it works …**

'Anthem for Doomed Youth' by Wilfred Owen:

> *Only the stuttering rifles' rapid rattle*
> *Can patter out their hasty orisons*

Here the 't' sounds mimic the sound of gunfire; the 'stuttering' sound is repeated twice in the two lines, helping to create a nervous atmosphere.

# Open Vowels

See: Long Vowels

# Oxymoron

**What is it?**
A two-word phrase bringing opposites together to express an idea (e.g. bitter sweet).

**What effect does it usually have?**
The use of an oxymoron implies that what is being described is unique and cannot be expressed in more ordinary words, or by using a single word.

**What else should I look out for?**
Because **oxymora** involve a seeming contradiction (how can something taste both bitter and sweet at the same time?) they are often used to express not only an ambivalent emotional state, but an ambiguous or irrational state of mind.

**An example of how it works …**
'Astrophel and Stella, VI' by Sir Philip Sidney:

> *Some lovers speak.*
> *..of heavenly beams infusing hellish pain,*
> *Of living deaths, dear wounds, fair storms, and freezing fires*

These lines capture the contradictory experience of love that causes extremes of pain and pleasure, making the lover feel both intensely alive and on the verge of death at the same time. The use of four oxymora in succession suggests the desperate madness of love.

**Another example …**
'Mental Cases' by Wilfred Owen:

> *what slow panic*
> *Gouged these chasms round their fretted sockets?*

Here the oxymoron 'slow panic' has an oneiric quality that captures the horrors on the battlefield that replay in slow motion within the minds of the injured soldiers.

# Parallelism

**What is it?**
Where a series of lines or phrases have a similar grammatical structure.

**What effect does it usually have?**
Parallelism usually makes a text feel orderly and elegantly balanced.

**What else should I look out for?**
Like anaphora, which may be thought of as a type of parallelism, this technique may be used to give a comprehensible structure to lengthy speeches; there are many examples in Shakespeare's history plays.

**An example of how it works …**
*Don Juan*, Canto II by Lord Byron:

> *She loved, and was beloved — she adored,*
> *And she was worshipped*

In these beautiful lines, the parallelism emphasises how the two lovers reciprocated perfectly, and neither loved or worshipped more than the other.

# Pararhyme

**What is it?**

Where the rhyming word (or syllable) has matching consonants but a different vowel sound (e.g. 'wells … walls' in Marlowe). Pararhyme may be considered a type of half-rhyme and is related to rich rhyme. Also called **frame rhyme** or **dissonantal rhyme** (as it is a rhyme that lacks the usual assonance).

**What effect does it usually have?**

Rhymes connect words together in order to reinforce meaning, or to make a contrast. Rhyming always emphasises words, but the second word of the rhyming pair, called the clinching word, carries more emphasis than the first.

**What else should I look out for?**

Like half-rhyme and eye rhyme, pararhyme tends to be used where full rhyming is considered too euphonious, too conspicuous, too conventional, or too obvious; it is often found internally as well as at line-end (e.g. 'And every moon made some or other mad').

**An example of how it works …**

'Futility' by Wilfred Owen:

> *Think how [the sun] wakes the seeds,—*
> *Woke, once, the clays of a cold star.*
> *Are limbs, so dear-achieved, are sides,*
> *Full-nerved—still warm—too hard to stir?*

The use of pararhyme, rather than full rhyme, complements the poem's restrained, sombre tone, as the bewildered soldier contemplates the lifeless body of his comrade.

**Another example …**

'Crisis is a Hair' by Emily Dickinson:

> *It—may jolt the Hand*
> *That adjusts the <u>Hair</u>*
> *That secures Eternity*
> *From presenting—<u>Here</u>—*

Here the pararhymes give greater emphasis to the aspirant of 'hand' to create a panting, fearsome quality, as the speaker contemplates the slight forces that attempt to hold the forces of death and destruction at bay.

# Personification

### What is it?

Where non-human things – animals, ideas or objects – are referred to as if they were human; e.g. when using the expression 'fortune favours the brave', good luck (fortune, an idea) is **personified**, since it is referred to as if it liked being generous to (favouring, a human action) those who have courage. Also called **prosopopoeia**.

### What effect does it usually have?

Personification enables poets to write about ideas in a more dramatic way, especially where ideas come into conflict with one another.

### What else should I look out for?

Where a number of ideas—or even a whole belief system—is presented in poetry, then it is not uncommon for personification to be used; **allegory** is where narrative poems are constructed from characters that are, effectively, **personified** ideas.

### An example of how it works …

'Sonnet 64' by William Shakespeare:

> *Time will come and take my love away*

Here, as in many other sonnets, the speaker uses personification to express his fear that eventually, at some point in the future, he will lose his 'love'. The use of personification dramatizes the struggle between time and love, making it a battle between the two forces that the reader may visualise. As with all metaphor, the personification also creates ambiguity: is he saying that time will destroy the emotion of love? or will it remove the beloved? and is this 'taking away' to be understood as permanent or temporary?

## Another example ...
*The Prelude* by William Wordsworth:

> *Oh Derwent, travelling over the green plains ...*
> *Mak[ing] ceaseless music through the night and day, ...*
> *giving me ... A knowledge ... of the calm*
> *Which Nature breathes among the fields and groves?*

First, the River Derwent is portrayed as a sort of musician; then Nature is presented as a sort of mother, breathing a lovely 'calm' over his infancy. The use of personification helps to convey the close relationship between the poet and the natural phenomena he is describing.

# Plosives

**What is it?**
Using a number of words close together containing plosives, the hardest consonants in English (*p, b, k, g, t* and *d* sounds). See Describing Sound in Poetry.

**What effect does it usually have?**
Plosives tend to sound tough, hard, strong, or heavy. They can help to convey anger, especially during dialogue.

**What else should I look out for?**
Settings described using many plosives tend to be harsh and unforgiving.

**An example of how it works ...**
'Sonnet 50' by William Shakespeare:

> *The beast that bears me, tired with my woe,*
> *Plods dully on, to bear that weight in me*

Here the poet describes a journey, away from his beloved; the many plosives, especially the 'b' and 'p' sounds, help to convey the horse's heavy plodding, as he rides with a leaden heart, knowing that 'grief' lies ahead of him, and 'joy' behind.

**Another example ...**
'During Wind and Rain' by Thomas Hardy:

> *Down their carved names the rain-drop ploughs*

Plosives work with nasals in this memorable phrase depicting how those who played joyfully in their youth are now lying cold and wet under the ground.

# Polyptoton

**What is it?**

Where a word is repeated in different forms (e.g. love, lover, lovable, loving, loved).

**What effect does it usually have?**

Polyptoton stresses the idea behind the repeated words (e.g. love), making it a key word, and connects words and phrases together.

**What else should I look out for?**

As well as emphasising ideas, polyptoton can affect the tone of the text, making it more intense, creating a sense of urgency; it can sometimes make the speaker seem obsessive.

**An example of how it works …**

*Astrophel and Stella*, XVI by Sir Philip Sidney:

> *I now have learned love right, and learned even so*
> *As they that being poisoned poison know*

In the preceding lines the speaker explains how, prior to falling in love himself, he thought lovers were like babies 'whining' about a pin prick. The polyptoton in the simile of the final line underlines the seriousness of his love for Stella, conveys the pain she causes him, and suggests he has been mortally wounded.

**Another example …**

'Sonnet 138' by William Shakespeare:

> *O, love's best habit is in seeming trust,*
> *And age in love loves not to have years told*

Here the poet is explaining why he and his 'dark lady' lie both to each other and to themselves: love requires at least the *appearance* of trust between lovers ('love's best habit'), and no ageing lover ('age in love') enjoys being reminded of his or her age. The word 'love' is repeated **polyptonically** in these lines to suggest that he is coming to terms with their dishonesty. In contrast to the anger he voices at the very start of the poem, where the phrase 'my love' is used with bitter sarcasm, the speaker is closer now to the sentiment of the couplet, where he accepts the lies as a sort of love-game they are playing together.

# Polysyndeton

**What is it?**
The use of 'and' repeatedly (or the use of another conjunction, such as 'but, 'or', etc.)

**What effect does it usually have?**
Polysyndeton quickens the pace; it heightens emotional intensity, especially approaching the climax of a poem.

**What else should I look out for?**
Using more conjunctions that usual can create a sense of innocent simplicity, since it may cause the style to resemble the speech of a child.

**An example of how it works …**
'The Angel' by William Blake:

> *And I wept both night and day,*
> *And he wiped my tears away;*
> *And I wept both day and night,*
> *And hid from him my heart's delight.*

In these lines the poet recalls a dream in which he was a 'maiden queen' watched over by 'an angel mild'. The use of polysyndeton, where 'and' is repeated anaphorically, gives the stanza a child-like innocence, and it works (with other repetitions) to bind the two rhyming couplets of the stanza together.

**Another example …**
'The Tint I Cannot Take' by Emily Dickinson:

> *And when I looked again—*
> *Nor Farm—nor Opal Herd—was there*
> *Nor Mediterranean*

The use of polysyndeton here creates an effective sense of closure, expressing the speaker's disappointment that her intensely colourful vision has faded back to normality.

# Present Participles

**What is it?**
Using the '-ing' form of verbs (e.g. 'he is running' rather than 'he runs'). Also called the **gerund**.

**What effect does it usually have?**
The present participle makes actions seem more dramatic, urgent or energetic.

**What else should I look out for?**
Many feminine line endings and feminine rhymes are formed using present participles.

**An example of how it works …**
'Dulce et Decorum Est' by Wilfred Owen:

> *Gas! GAS! Quick, boys!—An ecstasy of fumbling*
> *Fitting the clumsy helmets just in time,*
> *But someone still was yelling out and stumbling*
> *And floundering like a man in fire*

Here the drama of a gas attack is enhanced by the use of five present participles. The strong feminine rhyme on the words 'fumbling' and 'stumbling' emphasises these two words in particular, helping to deepen the pathos for this solder who dies horribly in front of us.

**Another example …**
*Don Juan*, Canto II by Lord Byron:

> *Drinking Salt-water like a mountain Stream,*
> *Tearing, and grinning, howling, screeching, swearing,*
> *And, with Hyæna laughter, died despairing*

The crazed behaviour of the sailors who resort to drinking sea water is emphasised by the string of present participles in the second line, rounded off with a grotesque image and a final present participle in the third.

# Proper Nouns

**What is it?**
Including **names** of people, places etc.

**What effect does it usually have?**
Proper nouns make a poem seem less generic, more about specific people or places; they impart a feeling of authenticity or realism.

**What else should I look out for?**
Names can have cultural, racial and social class connotations; some names are formal, others are nicknames, which affects tone. It is also worth thinking about where names are first used, especially if they are withheld earlier in the poem.

**An example of how it works …**
'The Chimney-Sweeper' by William Blake:

> *As Tom was a-sleeping, he had such a sight:*
> *That thousands of sweepers, Dick, Joe, Ned and Jack,*
> *Were all of them locked up in coffins of black*

Blake uses the poem to draw attention to the exploitation of children in eighteenth-century London: boys as young as five or six were being forced to work as chimney sweeps and suffering from incurable, crippling diseases. The fact that five boys are named makes it seem to refer to actual children, each an individual with a life that is worth saving.

# Prosopopoeia

See: Personification

# Quaesitio

**What is it?**
Asking a series of rhetorical questions, one after the other.

**What effect does it usually have?**
The piling up of questions creates a sense of urgency; the speaker is often made to seem unable to understand a situation, or in desperate need for answers.

**What else should I look out for?**
Quaesitio literally translates 'searching'; it tends to imply that the speaker is faced with an insoluble problem for which they seek a solution that never comes.

**An example of how it works …**
'The Tyger' by William Blake:

> *In what distant deeps or skies.*
> *Burnt the fire of thine eyes?*
> *On what wings dare he aspire?*
> *What the hand, dare seize the fire?*

In this stanza Blake confronts one of the great problems, that of the nature of God in a world containing violence and evil. The poem consists entirely of questions, none of which are answered.

**Another example …**
'My Beloved' by Langston Hughes:

> *Shall I make a record of your beauty?*
> *Shall I write words about you?*
> *Shall I make a poem that will live a thousand*
> *years and paint you in the poem?*

In this three-line poem, quaesitio is used to register not only the lover's longing, but his doubts about whether his poems can ever do justice to the beloved, and whether they will succeed in capturing and preserving her beauty.

# Repetition

See: Diacope

# Rhetorical Question

**What is it?**
A question asked to create an effect, rather than for an answer.

**What effect does it usually have?**
Rhetorical questions are often used as a method of persuasion; the implication is that anyone in their right mind needs no answer to the question.

**What else should I look out for?**
Rhetorical questions can create a sense of entreaty, or a pleading tone, especially when they are used one after the other (a technique called **quaesitio**). They are also used to present a topic to be further explored in the text, such as in the famous opening line, 'Shall I compare thee to a summer's day?'

**An example of how it works ...**
'The Schoolboy' by William Blake:

> *How can the bird that is born for joy*
> *Sit in a cage and sing?*

Here the writer uses a rhetorical question to convey the immorality of confining children to 'cruel' and 'dreary' schools; no bird can sing for long in a cage, it is argued, just as no child can keep their 'youthful spring' in that environment.

**Another example ...**
'Ode to the West Wind' by P. B. Shelley:

> *O Wind*
> *If Winter comes, can Spring be far behind?*

The poet closes this poem expressing hope that the oppressions of the present – symbolised by winter – will eventually pass. The rhetorical question makes the speaker's longing for a brighter future seem both more heartfelt and tentative.

# Rich Rhyme

**What is it?**
Where the two rhyming words are homophones, matching
exactly. (The term is not applied to the repetition of a word.)
Also known by the French term, **rime riche**.

**What effect does it usually have?**
Because rich rhyme are rare and difficult to write, they tend
to occur in isolation; this gives them greater emphasis than
the more common forms of rhyme. They invariably bring
with them a sense of showmanship, often involving the use
of ingenious puns.

**What else should I look out for?**
Rich rhyme is found far more often in languages like French,
or in Medieval poetry; some writers therefore use them when
evoking (or imitating) distant poets.

**An example of how it works …**
'General Prologue to the Canterbury Tales' by Geoffrey
Chaucer:

> *The hooly blisful martir for to seke,*
> *That hem hath holpen whan that they were seke*

Here the poet refers to the reason for the pilgrims' journey:
to 'seke' the holy martyr (the shrine of Thomas à Becket),
who helps them when they are 'seke' (sick). The rich rhyme
neatly brings the opening verse-paragraph of the poem to a
close. The notion of healing, in terms of redemption,
becomes especially important later in the text; the poem
ends, in fact, with *The Parson's Tale* - a homily on the subject
of penitence.

**Another example …**

'Sonnet 135' by William Shakespeare:

> *So thou, being rich in Will, add to thy Will*
> *One will of mine to make thy large Will more.*
> *Let 'no' unkind no fair beseechers kill:*
> *Think all but one, and me in that one Will*

The poet puns on his name throughout this poem. The rich rhyme that occurs at the end serves to intensify the (for modern readers) infuriating effect.

# Rime Riche

See: Rich Rhyme

# Rocking Lineation

### What is it?
Running a series of pentameters (or hexameters) caesura to caesura, so that they flow across enjambed lines and stop/start mid-line. Rocking lineation usually occurs in blank verse poems, other narrative verse, and dramatic verse, especially longer speeches by Shakespeare and his contemporaries.

### What effect does it usually have?
Rocking lineation gives verse greater variety, helping to prevent longer stretches becoming repetitive or predictable. As with other irregular verse features, it creates a subtle tension and then a relief when standard, end-stopped lineation returns.

### What else should I look out for?
Some commentators discuss rocking lineation being in 'counterpoint' with the usual poetic unit, the lines themselves. Poets might slip between conventional lineation and rocking lineation to create various dramatic effects, for contrast, or to build towards a particularly significant line (e.g. by establishing a pattern of rocking lineation and then writing a series of rushing, enjambed lines followed by an end stop on a key phrase).

### An example of how it works …
*The Prelude* by William Wordsworth:

> *So sweetly 'mid the gloom the invisible bird*
> *Sang to itself that there I could have made*
> *My dwelling-place, and lived for ever there*
> *To hear such music. Through the walls we flew*
> *And down the valley, and, a circuit made*

> *In wantonness of heart, through rough and smooth*
> *We scampered homeward.*

Here the poet describes reluctantly riding away from an idyllic spot – a ruined abbey in which a single wren 'sang so sweetly'. The rocking lineation (which is seen most clearly in the pentameter running from the first full stop to 'valley') gives this moment of the narrative a lively quality that conveys how energised and renewed he was by his encounter with the bird.

# Rhyme

**What is it?**
Everyone knows a rhyme when they see it. Technically, two syllables rhyme when their vowels and the following consonant (if there is one) sounds the same. Where needed to distinguish it from other types of rhyme, this may be called **full rhyme** or **masculine rhyme**.

**What effect does it usually have?**
Rhymes connect words together in order to reinforce meaning, or to make a contrast. **Rhyming** always emphasises words, but the second word of the rhyming pair, called the **clinching** word, carries more emphasis than the first.

**What else should I look out for?**
Together with metre and its organisation into lines (lineation), rhyme is one of the most important ways in which poems are given a sense of order and harmony, elevating poetry above the randomness of everyday speech. Reading a rhyming poem of usual length creates a sense of expectation from the reader; when a rhyme is missing – or a half rhyme used in its place – the impact is always worth exploring.

**An example of how it works …**
'La Belle Dame Sans Merci' by John Keats:

> *I met a lady in the meads,*
> *Full beautiful—a faery's child,*
> *Her hair was long, her foot was light,*
> *And her eyes were wild*

In this stanza the knight recounts meeting his 'dame', a *femme fatale* who will go on to enslave him. The rhyme creates a contrast between the innocent-sounding 'child' with the dangerous-sounding 'wild'; this helps to reinforce our first impression of this alluring 'lady', outwardly attractive but bewitching and malevolent.

# Rhyming Couplet

**What is it?**
Two consecutive lines that rhyme.

**What effect does it usually have?**
A couplet will create a strong sense of closure at the end of a stanza or poem using a different rhyme scheme; the rhyme tends to be more noticeable than where cross-rhyming is used (since the rhymes are closer together) creating a sense of wit or polish.

**What else should I look out for?**
An **heroic couplet** is a rhyming couplet written in iambic pentameter; these tend to call to mind the poetry of Dryden and Pope, much of which was written in imitation of classical models.

**An example of how it works …**
'Sonnet 29' by William Shakespeare:

> *For thy sweet love remembered such wealth brings*
> *That then I scorn to change my state with kings*

These two lines bring the sonnet to a satisfying conclusion, conveying love's power to exalt with a fresh and powerful metaphor.

# Semi-Rhyme

See: Half-Rhyme

# Short Line

**What is it?**
A line significantly shorter than neighbouring lines; a line of about six syllables or less.

**What effect does it usually have?**
Short lines tend to quicken the pace; they make lines feel lighter and more energetic, and in some cases are reminiscent of the nursery rhyme or hymn.

**What else should I look out for?**
Sometimes a stanza will have a line that is much shorter than the others, called a **bob line**; this can have a humorous effect, or can be used to create other effects.

**An example of how it works …**
'Spring' by William Blake:

> *Little Lamb*
> *Here I am,*
> *Come and lick*
> *My white neck.*
> *Let me pull*
> *Your soft Wool.*
> *Let me kiss*
> *Your soft face*

The very short lines of this poem help to capture the joy and innocence of a children and lambs in springtime; Blake uses such scenes to contrast with the dark world of urban 'experience' found in texts such as 'The Chimney Sweeper'.

**Another example …**
'At Castle Boterel' by Thomas Hardy:

> *I look back at it amid the rain*
> *For the very last time; for my sand is sinking,*
> *And I shall traverse old love's domain*
> *Never again*

The bob-line at the end of this stanza creates a poignant sense of time running out, or life being cut short. The poet reflects on how he is too old to travel in 'love's domain': he will never return to Cornwall, where he fell in love with Emma as a young man, or he will never love again, or both.

# Sibilance

**What is it?**
Using a number of words close together containing sibilant consonants (s, z, sh sounds).

**What effect does it usually have?**
Sibilance literally means 'hissing'. This sound can be used to convey a threat or create a sinister atmosphere; for snarling or insane dialogue (e.g. the mad Ferdinand says 'I'll find scorpions to string my whips' in Webster); for whispering ; or onomatopoeically to mimic the sound hissing air or running water ('sweet seasoned showers' in Shakespeare).

**What else should I look out for?**
Poets often use sibilance in a more general way, alongside other forms of consonance, to create a sense of harmony.

**An example of how it works ...**
'Exposure' by Wilfred Owen:

> *Sudden successive flights of bullets streak the silence.*

The onomatopoeic sibilance of this line enables the reader to hear, as well as see, the bullets tearing through the freezing air.

**Another example ...**
'Proud Songsters' by Thomas Hardy:

> *the finches whistle in ones and pairs*

The poet's use of sibilance mimics the high notes made by the birds as well as the light-hearted beauty of the scene, where the birds seem to be singing solos and duets.

# Sight Rhyme

See: Eye Rhyme

# Simile

### What is it?
Where one thing or action is said to be 'like' or 'as' another.

### What effect does it usually have?
Similes enable the poet to bring imagery into the text to visualise ideas or feelings; as well as being decorative, this imagery may engage the reader and makes the language used to express the ideas richer and more suggestive or ambiguous.

### What else should I look out for?
Likening one thing to another makes a connection between them which may be deeper than it seems at first sight; e.g. 'I wandered lonely as a cloud' conveys more than just loneliness, since the poet is presenting himself as free and at one with the natural landscape he is travelling.

### An example of how it works …
'Sonnet 97' by William Shakespeare:

> *How like a winter hath my absence been*
> *From thee …*
> *What freezings have I felt, what dark days seen*

In these lines Shakespeare uses a simile to liken the pain of separation with the discomfort and lifelessness of winter; this enables him to flatteringly compare the beloved to summer, and exploit the various associations of these two seasons.

# Slant Rhyme

See: Half-Rhyme

# Spondee

**What is it?**
When two syllables are stressed, one after the other. See
Understanding Versification.

**What effect does it usually have?**
Spondees are used to emphasise important words and
images.

**What else should I look out for?**
Spondees are often found alongside other features of
irregular verse (enjambment, caesura, or feminine line-
endings) or alongside hard consonants, creating a rough
texture; hyphenation usually results in a spondee.

**An example of how it works …**
'Sonnet 73' by William Shakespeare:

> *leaves … do hang*
> *Upon those boughs which shake against the cold,*
> *Bare ruin'd choirs, where late the sweet birds sang*

In these lines where seasonal imagery is used to contrast past
and present, the **spondaic** line opening ('Bare ruined …')
places heavy emphasis on the image of the leafless, birdless
tree, a potent symbol for the speaker's depressing emotional
and physical state.

**Another example …**
'Mental Cases' by Wilfred Owen:

> *Sunlight seems a blood-smear; night comes blood-black*

Here spondees are used to emphasise the two key images of the line, both beginning with the word 'blood': the shell-shocked veterans see gore wherever they look, it is implied; the horror of battle is inescapable, even when they are hundreds of miles from the front.

# Spondaic Line Opening

See: Spondee and Understanding Versification.

# Syllepsis

See: Zeugma

# Superlative

### What is it?
Grammatical term for the type of adjective or adverb ending in '-est' (brightest, fastest, best, etc.)

### What effect does it usually have?
Like comparatives, superlatives are often used to reinforce a sense of excellence; they are therefore frequently used when praising (or flattering) a loved one, or when invoking a divinity.

### What else should I look out for?
Superlatives are sometimes hyperbolic, to suggest that the poet is overcome with admiration.

### An example of how it works …
'Ode to Psyche' by John Keats:

> *O latest born and loveliest vision far*
> *Of all Olympus' faded hierarchy! ... O brightest!*

Keats uses the superlatives in these lines to show reverence to Psyche, a goddess not worshipped in the ancient world (since she was created by Apuleius, a second-century Roman author) but whose beauty nonetheless outshines the 'faded' gods of the past.

### Another example …
'Sonnet 35' by William Shakespeare:

> *Roses have thorns, and silver fountains mud ...*
> *And loathsome canker lives in sweetest bud*

Whilst professing to reassure the beloved that his 'sensual fault' (presumably infidelity) is forgiven, the strength of the superlative, especially coming after the blunt monosyllable of 'mud', suggests that there is a subtext of disgust, both at human weakness and at himself.

# Synaesthesia

### What is it?
A type of metaphor where the experience of one sense is described in terms of a different sense; we use **synaesthetic** metaphors in everyday speech (e.g. bitter cold).

### What effect does it usually have?
In poetry, synaesthesia has the effect of intensifying the experience being portrayed in the text; it can often create an unreal, dream-like atmosphere.

### What else should I look out for?
A sense of wonder often accompanies synaesthesia. Familiar sensations can be made to seem new or strange, as if a child were experiencing them for the first time; this is what literary theorists call defamiliarization.

### An example of how it works …
'The Taxi' by Amy Lowell:

> *the lamps of the city prick my eyes*
> *So that I can no longer see your face.*
> *Why should I leave you,*
> *To wound myself upon the sharp edges of the night?*

Here the lights of the city are described in terms of touch to convey the intense pain of separation experienced by the speaker.

# Syncope

See: Elision

# Synecdoche

**What is it?**
Where the part of something is used to refer to the whole of
it (e.g. 'three mouths to feed', to mean 'three children').

**What effect does it usually have?**
Synecdoche is used in poems to create striking imagery.

**What else should I look out for?**
Technically, synecdoche is a type of metonymy; it is often
used to draw attention to particular body parts.

**An example of how it works …**
'I've Nothing Else' by Emily Dickinson:

> *the Night keeps fetching Stars*
> *To our familiar eyes*

Here the poet uses a synecdoche to refer to the way that
humankind usually takes stars for granted – until they fail to
appear, and we lose our way.

**Another example …**
'Jerusalem' by William Blake:

> *And did those feet in ancient time,*
> *Walk upon England's mountains green?*

Here Blake refers to the belief, common at one time, that
Christ once visited the British Isles; referring to his feet
makes him sound innocent and humble, both calling to mind
the stories of feet-washing from the Bible, and reinforcing
the Holy Lamb of God image in the following lines.

# Tricolon

**What is it?**
A three-part structure, where each word or phrase is of roughly equal length; a three-part list. More loosely, the term is sometimes used to refer to a triad, or the rule of three.

**What effect does it usually have?**
As every advertiser and politician knows, tricolons have a unique power, rendering phrases more memorable, neater or more resonant.

**What else should I look out for?**
Tricolons tend to make the expression of ideas more concise, where relatively complex ideas are compressed into the three-unit form.

**An example of how it works …**
'Stopping by Woods on a Snowy Evening' by Robert Frost:

> *The woods are lovely, dark and deep*

The temptation felt by the speaker to linger in the snowy woods, which has already been described in some detail, is summarised using a neat tricolon in the final stanza of the poem.

**Another example …**
'Ode to a Nightingale' by John Keats:

> *The weariness, the fever, and the fret*
> *Here, where … palsy shakes a few, sad, last grey hairs,*
> *Where youth grows pale, and spectre-thin, and dies*

These two despairing tricolons express the pain of mortal life for the speaker, underlining the urgency of his desire to fly away with the nightingale, who exists in an entirely different realm; as he says in another resonant tricolon, to 'Fade far away, dissolve, and quite forget' what the bird has 'never known'.

# Transferred Epithet

**What is it?**
Where an adjective (epithet) is detached from the thing it is actually describing, and given to a nearby noun in the sentence. Also called **hypallage**.

**What effect does it usually have?**
Transferred epithets can be more concise, leading to a sense of concentration in the text and make the language seem fresh, new or surprising.

**What else should I look out for?**
Sometimes transferred epithets enable a poet to apply an adjective to two nouns simultaneously.

**An example of how it works ...**
'Dulce et Decorum Est' by Wilfred Owen:

> *Gas! GAS! Quick, boys!—An ecstasy of fumbling*
> *Fitting the clumsy helmets just in time*

Here referring to the helmets as 'clumsy' is more a concise and elegant choice than saying 'fitting the helmets clumsily', which is a less interesting phrase.

**Another example ...**
*The Prelude* by William Wordsworth:

> *by the margin of the trembling lake*
> *Beneath the gloomy hills I homeward went*

In a passage dealing with the speaker's love and fearsome respect for the power of nature, the adjective 'trembling' seems to refer both to him and to the lake; likewise 'gloomy', since he is reluctant to return home and leave the natural world.

# Triple Rhyme

**What is it?**
Where words rhyme on three syllables.

**What effect does it usually have?**
Because triple rhymes are rare and comparatively difficult to write, they tend to occur in isolation; this gives them greater emphasis than the more common forms of rhyme. Like double and feminine rhymes, triple rhymes may be used for comic effect, and tend to bring with them a sense of showmanship or ingenuity.

**What else should I look out for?**
Triple rhyme is found far more often in languages like Italian, or in Medieval poetry; some writers therefore use them when evoking (or imitating) distant poets.

**An example of how it works …**
'The Nun's Priest's Tale' by Geoffrey Chaucer:

> *Swevenes engendren of replecciouns,*
> *And ofte of fume and of complecciouns*

Here Pertelote delivers a haughty lecture to Chanticleer, telling him off for allowing himself to be frightened by dreams, which are simply caused by overeating. The triple rhyme draws attention to her medical terminology, helping to present her, comically, as a learned authority on such matters—she is a farmyard hen, after all!

**Another example …**
*Don Juan*, Canto II by Lord Byron:

> *Then he himself sunk down all dumb and Shivering,*
> *And gave no sign of life, save his limbs quivering*

With this triple rhyme at the end of a painful couplet, a child dies in the arms of his father. As well as placing emphasis on the verbs used to depict the boy's death throes, the triple rhyme seems to have been used by Byron in imitation of Dante: this passage was inspired by the depiction of Ugolino, who is punished by starvation in *The Inferno*.

# Trochee

See: Understanding Versification

# Trochaic Line Opening

See: Understanding Versification

# Verbless Sentence

**What is it?**

A sentence of more than a few words' length not containing a verb.

**What effect does it usually have?**

The absence of verbs places greater emphasis on the imagery of the sentence.

**What else should I look out for?**

Removing verbs from a sentence has the effect of removing tense, leaving the images hovering in a timeless space. Verblessness can also create ambiguity.

**An example of how it works …**

*The Cantos*, IV by Ezra Pound:

> *Spotted stag of the wood;*
> *Gold, gold, a sheaf of hair*

The lack of verbs, here as elsewhere in the text, helps the poet to evoke the distant world of Greek myth. The poet is evoking the death of Actaeon by presenting us with two close-ups: the unfortunate hunter's newly-grown deerskin and the golden hair of the Diana, representing her beauty, purity, and divinity.

# Vernacular

See: Dialect

# White Space

**What is it?**
Where short lines and or short stanzas are used, leaving white space on the printed page.

**What effect does it usually have?**
White space creates a lighter or an emptier feel about the poem.

**What else should I look out for?**
It is often worth comparing how the poem feels on the page with those before or after it in the collection; often poets position such texts between others with far longer lines, to accentuate the effect.

**An example of how it works ...**
'Where the Picnic Was' by Thomas Hardy:

> *Now a cold wind blows,*
> *And the grass is grey,*
> *But the spot still shows*
> *As a burnt circle ...*

Here the poet has chosen to use short lines divided into three stanzas; in most editions there is also a gap after the poem on the printed page. The ample white space helps to convey the speaker's loneliness, despair and emptiness now that he has lost the company of those who picnicked with him at the place he has visited, during far happier times.

# Zeugma

**What is it?**
Where a verb is given two objects, to which it carries different meanings. Also called **syllepsis**.

**What effect does it usually have?**
Zeugma tends to be amusing and helps to portray the writer as witty and sophisticated.

**What else should I look out for?**
Like a good chiasmus, a witty zeugma is not easy to write. Zeugmas therefore tend to make texts more impressive; they may also make certain phrases more striking and memorable.

**An example of how it works …**
'The Rape of the Lock, Canto II' by Alexander Pope:

> *Or lose her heart, or necklace, at a ball*

Here the verb 'lose' is used **zeugmatically**, since to lose one's heart means 'to fall in love', whereas to lose one's necklace simply means to misplace it. This implies that valuable jewellery are just as important as love to the girls Pope is describing.

**Another example …**
*Don Juan*, Canto II by Lord Byron:

> *There's nought, no doubt, so much the spirit calms*
> *As rum and true religion*

To 'calm the spirit' by means of prayer and contemplation of the Bible is clearly very different to 'calming' oneself with a bottle of rum but, by using zeugma to connect them, Byron expresses his cynical mistrust of religious devotion, suggesting that worship is self-indulgent and escapist, rather like drinking spirits.

# Five Poetic Principles

It's never a good idea to approach a poem with a list of features or devices to look for; this tends to lead to mechanical, 'forced' responses. Nevertheless, sometimes it's good to have some help generating ideas, at the planning stage.

These **poetic principles** are not features to spot, but important aspects of the way poetry works. Get used to finding evidence for each of them, and you will present yourself as a sensitive, intelligent, experienced and well-informed reader.

### Beauty
Remember to talk about the beauty of particular lines or phrases. Poems are not just intended to communicate ideas and feelings; still less are they designed for students to analyse. Poets intend us to admire them as aesthetic objects in their own right, rather like a painting hanging on a gallery wall, or a perfectly-crafted vase.

### Resonance
Resonance is a special quality that separates great literature from cheap paperbacks, poetry from advertising rhymes. The best poems are more than just memorable; they resonate within us in a deep and long-lasting way. The *Oxford Dictionary* defines resonance as the power to evoke enduring images, memories, and emotions.

**Ambiguity**

The difficulty we often have in being certain about how to interpret poems should be acknowledged: ambiguity and ambivalence add richness and complexity to literary works, making them fascinating and enigmatic, so that we experience them in different ways when we revisit them over time. Ambiguity concerns meaning, and ambivalence feelings.

**Iconicity**

A text is said to have iconicity when its form reflects its content. Ask yourself, in other words, if *the way the poem is written* imitates (or otherwise helps to convey) what is being written *about*. It usually does in the best poems. Onomatopoeia is one form of iconicity, but pace, structure, and many other features can be involved.

**Dichotomy**

Literary works (indeed, all languages) create meaning through binary oppositions or dichotomies. Look beyond contrasting imagery to try and identify a key underlying opposition in the poem's theme (e.g. youth vs. age, new vs. old, war vs. peace, truth vs. lies, good vs. evil, innocence vs. experience).

To help you remember these principles, think of the word B.R.A.I.D. and how these ideas may be elegantly woven in your essay!

# Describing Sound in Poetry

Poems are, of course, made of words; words are made of syllables; syllables are made of a combination of vowel and (usually) consonant sounds.

To fully appreciate any poem, some attention needs to be paid to **syllables**, the building blocks of language. Without doing that, we cannot appreciate the rhythm of the poem, or the effects produced by the sounds that it makes.

Analysing the sounds of a poem usually involves identifying **repeated patterns**: the main devices are rhyme, alliteration, assonance, consonance, and sibilance. Poets tend to choose words that match others of the poem instinctively, creating a sense of the language fitting together, or being in harmony. One way of judging the quality of unrhymed poetry is by analysing its sounds: the best poems written in English use a subset of the 50+ sounds available in the language, just as artists will often repeat colours and use a palette of a small number of shades in their paintings.

Different sounds, like different colours, have **implications** in themselves. They may seem blunt and harsh; soft and gentle; redolent of water or of wind.

Within a line of poetry, sounds can also give particular words more **impact**. Tom Paulin (see below) writes of how sound and metre work together in these lines: 'Grief melts away, / Like <u>snow</u> in May, / As if there were <u>no</u> such <u>cold</u> thing.' As well as the rhyme on the first two lines, assonance connects the three underlined words, giving special emphasis to 'cold', whose hard sound not only suits the word's meaning but contrasts with the softer preceding sounds.

Vowel sounds have a particularly important role to play in giving control over the **pace** of the poem. They may look similar on the page but some vowels are many times longer than others. Compare the vowels of the words 'sit' and 'sea', for example.

## Terminology

Although there are many technical terms available for describing and categorising consonant sounds,* the most useful are:

> *Plosives* [ $p$ - $b$ - $t$ - $d$ - $k$ - $g$ ]
> The hardest sounds of English;
>
> *Gutturals* [ $k$ - $g$ ]
> The hardest of the plosives;
>
> *Fricatives* [ $f$ - $v$ - $th$ - $s$ - $z$ - $sh$ - $j$ ]
> The soft, breathy sounds;
>
> *Sibilants* [ $s$ - $z$ - $sh$ ]
> The hissing or whispering fricatives;
>
> *Nasals* [ $m$ - $n$ ]
> The humming or 'this is tasty' sounds;
>
> *Aspirants* [ $h$ ]
> The sound of breathing out.

Remember it's the *sounds* not the *spelling* that matters. So the word 'physical' starts with a fricative, not with a plosive, since the first two letters sound like an *f*.

* e.g. labial, dental, labio-dental, alveolar, etc. These, and many other terms, are used by linguists to refer to the location and method of consonant production in the mouth and throat. We don't need to worry about them!

Further Reading:

*The Secret Life of Poems* by Tom Paulin
Up-close discussion of a range of poems, with
extensive analysis of the impact of sound choices in
particular lines: 'This is how poetry works. As
Robert Frost said, "the ear does it."

*The Art of Shakespeare's Sonnets* by Helen Vendler
Incredibly detailed analysis of all 154 sonnets,
including texts and diagrams; each of the poems is
said to have a 'couplet tie' which binds the last two
lines to earlier lines by means of sounds and 'key
words'.

# Understanding Versification

Rhythm in poetry, which is called **metre**, may be organised in different ways, which is called **versification**, the making of 'verses'.

In order to do this, poets working in English choose and re-order words in ways that take advantage of the inherent rhythms of the language.

When we speak English, we say some syllables louder than others. For example, in the word 'advantage', the middle syllable must be spoken more loudly than the first and third. (A good dictionary will tell you that is how the word *has to be* pronounced.) When talking about versification, we call the louder syllables **stressed** and the relatively quieter ones **unstressed**. These are the elements that poets organise to create different metres in their work, with the **stresses** acting as the equivalent of beats in music.

If we now take a line of poetry, we can see how this works in a whole line:

> O *never say* that *I* was *false* of *heart*.

The word '*never*' must be pronounced with the **stress** on the first syllable, and most speakers would pronounce the words 'say', 'I', 'false', and 'heart' a little more loudly than the neighbouring syllables; these are the words that carry most of the line's meaning—a word like 'that' is grammatically necessary, but communicates nothing by itself.

What makes versification in English tricky is that there is an element of personal judgement involved. We *could*, if we wanted to, make 'was' the loudest syllable in the line. Whilst this would not be 'wrong', poets expect readers to exercise their own judgement.

**Metres**

Iambic metre is by far the most common in English, but it's worth knowing about the other main ones too:

> *Iambic* [ unstressed > stressed ]
> e.g. the word 'he<u>llo</u>' is iambic;
>
> *Trochaic* [ *stressed > unstressed* ]
> e.g. the word '<u>so</u>rry' is trochaic;
>
> *Anapaestic* [ *unstressed > unstressed > stressed* ]
> e.g. the word 'unaware' is anapaestic;
>
> *Dactylic* [ *stressed > unstressed > unstressed* ]
> e.g. the word 'easily' is dactylic.

In order to describe the metre fully, one of the above words is then combined with another referring to how many of stresses there are to the line.

The most common are:

> *Hexameter*: 6 stresses
>
> *Pentameter*: 5 stresses
>
> *Tetrameter*: 4 stresses
>
> *Trimeter*: 3 stresses
>
> *Dimeter*: 2 stresses.

So now we can say with confidence that the line of verse quoted above is in iambic pentameter.

**Irregular Verse**

Sometimes poets write in very **regular metre**, as in this line:

*When I do count the clock that tells the time.*

Here Shakespeare opens his poem with an entirely regular
line (providing 'I' is stressed, rather than 'when', which is
what makes sense) to imitate the ticking of a clock.
More usually, poets use a mixture of regular and irregular
lines of verse for the sake of variety. The beating of iambic
verse is often compared to the beating of the heart; when
something particularly exciting happens, this heartbeat
becomes irregular. Normally when we write about verse in
poems, we are commenting on the irregular features, and the
effect that they have.

In iambic pentameter (as in a Shakespeare play, for instance),
the irregular features most often worth discussing are:

> *Spondee*
> Where two stresses occur in a row (a *spondaic*
> phrase);

> *Molossus*
> Where three stresses occur in a row (a *molossian*
> phrase);

> *Trochaic line opening*
> Where the first two syllables are *trochaic* rather than
> iambic;

> *Spondaic line opening*
> Where the first two syllables are *spondaic* (stressed)
> rather than iambic;

*Pyrrhic line opening*
Where the first two syllables are *pyrrhic* (unstressed) rather than iambic;

*Feminine line ending*
Where an extra unstressed syllable occurs at the end of the line.

Alongside these features, it is typical to find caesura and enjambment, leading to a general sense of disorder or loss of control in the structure of the verse. All of these features are discussed, with examples, among the other poetic devices of Poetry Hacks.

Further Reading:

*The Poetry Handbook* by John Lennard
Contains an excellent chapter on verse and how it works in English, along with a range of examples, comprehensive glossaries and exercises.

*How to Read a Poem* by Terry Eagleton
Contains a witty and common-sense discussion under the subheading 'Rhythm and Metre'. This was first published by *The Times* newspaper, and is available online to subscribers; Google 'How to Read a Poem: Part Three' and you will find it.

# Verbs to Use in Your Essays

A great way to make your poetry essays more impressive is by using some of the following verbs. Words that may be used in similar situations have been grouped together.

Top tip: ban the words 'show' and 'display' completely, and use some of these words instead …

> e.g.
> The poet uses this phrase to **emphasise** / **highlight** / **underline** / **stress** / **foreground** / **affirm** the importance of the freedom of speech.

> e.g.
> The diction of this stanza **suggests** / **evokes** / **conjures** (up) the carefree world of early childhood.

> e.g.
> The poem's dark imagery **heightens** / **intensifies** / **magnifies** / **accentuates** / **amplifies** / **deepens** / **reinforces** / **compounds** its profound sense of grief.

> e.g.
> The short lines and simple metre **recall** / **call to mind** / **are reminiscent** of / **are redolent** of nursery rhymes.

> e.g.
> The chaotic structure in this part of the poem **echoes** / **mimics** / **mirrors** / **reflects** / **replicates** / **enacts** / **dramatizes** the speaker's quickly worsening mental state.

e.g.

The poem vividly **presents** / **portrays** / **depicts** / **sketches** / **captures** / **embodies** / **visualises** / **pictures** / **delineates** the joy of parenthood.

e.g.

The speaker compares the cruel landowners to wolves in order to clearly **express** / **convey** / **voice** / **register** / **signify** / **give expression** to his contempt for them.

e.g.

The drooping flowers **symbolise** / **represent** / **stand for** / **betoken** / **are an emblem** of / **are emblematic** of their dying love affair.

e.g.

The soft sounds of the poem **impart** / **lend** / **give** / **endow it** with / **bestow upon** it / **establish** a welcoming, unthreatening atmosphere.

e.g.

The poem's quickening pace enables the writer to **elicit** / **draw** / **provoke** a sense of anxiety from the reader / **share** his increasing anxiety with the reader.

# Adjectives from A to V

The following adjectives, from **A**uthentic to **V**ivid, can be used in different ways when writing about poems and indeed other types of text.

Note that the words in each group have slightly different meanings, though they can often be used in similar situations.

**Authentic**
Spontaneous
Genuine
Sincere
Convincing

**Chaotic**
Disorderly
Arbitrary
Incongruous
Fragmented
Jarring

**Concise**
Succinct
Intense
Dense
Concentrated
Pithy
Terse

**Crowded**
Cluttered
Claustrophobic

**Elegant**
Well-crafted
Delicate
Sophisticated

**Energetic**
Dynamic
Animated
Lively
Pacey
Fluent

**Expressive**
Emotive
Moving
Profound
Poignant

**Fresh**
Unique
Original

**Lucid**
Perceptive
Penetrating
Astute
Clear-sighted
Crystalline
Pellucid

**Lyrical**
Musical
Harmonious
Mellifluous
Delightful
Euphonious
Pleasing
Soothing
Comforting
Memorable

**Measured**
Balanced
Poised
Rational
Reasonable
Logical
Cohesive

**Suggestive**
Rich
Ambivalent
Evocative

**Unsettling**
Disturbing
Discomforting
Provocative
Surprising
Striking

**Vivid**
Graphic
Vibrant
Arresting
Engaging
Compelling
Resonant

# About Poetry Hacks

Yes, I can see that's alliteration … *but what does it do?*

**Poetry Hacks** came about as a way of helping my literature students answer that sort of question. Most of them find it easy to go through a poem and spot a good handful of features – enough to write an essay – but the next step often had them stuck.

*How to Read a Poem*, *How Poetry Works* … Most of the bluffer's guides to poetry out there take the same approach: they consist of a series of commentaries; typically, each chapter explores one of the author's favourite poems. There is much to learn from such books, but my students needed a book that started with the features, rather than the poems; and they had deadlines. They needed quick answers.

The usual theory is that perceptive readers need to be left alone to 'feel' the poem for themselves, but time and again the questions kept coming up, even with my best students: What can I say about assonance? What does rhyme do? When I started to think about it, I realised that experience had an important role to play: after a number of years in the business, we learn what to look for.

Thus Poetry Hacks was born, an Android app, then a Kindle book, now a paperback especially for students staring at the page, quick hacks to help them *get on with writing the essay.*

The examples are drawn from poets whose work is out of copyright and in the public domain. I have modernised spellings where possible, for the sake of readability.

Example poets (so far):

Alexander Pope, Amy Lowell, Christopher Marlowe, D. H. Lawrence, Edmund Spenser, Emily Dickinson, Ezra Pound, Geoffrey Chaucer, John Keats, Katherine Mansfield, Langston Hughes, Lord Byron, P. B. Shelley, Samuel Taylor Coleridge, Sir Philip Sidney, Thomas Hardy, Wilfred Owen, William Blake, William Shakespeare, William Wordsworth.

# About the Author

J. E. Clapham was educated at Edinburgh University and Worcester College, Oxford. He has been Head of English at St Edward's Oxford for over ten years, teaching English Literature both for A-level and for the International Baccalaureate.

Printed in Great Britain
by Amazon